T0076195

Get the eBook FREE!

(PDF, ePub, Kindle, and liveBook all included)

We believe that once you buy a book from us, you should be able to read it in any format we have available. To get electronic versions of this book at no additional cost to you, purchase and then register this book at the Manning website.

Go to https://www.manning.com/freebook and follow the instructions to complete your pBook registration.

That's it!
Thanks from Manning!

Praise for the First Edition

"This book does the impossible: it makes math fun and easy!"

—Sander Rossel, COAS Software Systems

"Do you want to treat yourself to learning algorithms in the same way that you would read your favorite novel? If so, this is the book you need!"

—Sankar Ramanathan, IBM Analytics

"In today's world, there is no aspect of our lives that isn't optimized by some algorithm. Let this be the first book you pick up if you want a well-explained introduction to the topic."

—Amit Lamba, Tech Overture, LLC

"Algorithms are not boring! This book was fun and insightful for both my students and me."

—Christopher Haupt, Mobirobo, Inc

grokking
algorithms

Second Edition

Aditya Y. Bhargava

Foreword by Daniel Zingaro

MANNING
SHELTER ISLAND

Manning Publications Co.
20 Baldwin Road
Shelter Island, NY 11964

Development editor: Ian Hough
Technical editor: David Eisenstat
Review editor: Aleksandar Dragosavljević
Production editor: Andy Marinkovich
Copy editor: Alisa Larson
Proofreader: Jason Everett
Technical proofreader: Tony Holdroyd
Typesetter: Dennis Dalinnik
Cover designer: Leslie Haimes

ISBN 9781633438538
Printed in the United States of America

· ·

For my parents, Sangeeta and Yogesh

brief contents

1	introduction to algorithms	1
2	selection sort	21
3	recursion	41
4	quicksort	55
5	hash tables	77
6	breadth-first search	101
7	trees	121
8	balanced trees	141
9	Dijkstra's algorithm	165
10	greedy algorithms	191
11	dynamic programming	203
12	k-nearest neighbors	229
13	where to go next	247

contents

foreword   xiii

preface   xv

acknowledgments   xvii

about this book   xix

about the author   xxiii

1   introduction to algorithms   **1**

Binary search   3
Big O notation   10

2   selection sort   **21**

How memory works   22
Arrays and linked lists   24
Which is used more, arrays or linked lists?   31
Selection sort   34
Example code listing   38

3 recursion 41

Recursion 42
Base case and recursive case 44
The stack 46

4 quicksort 55

Divide and conquer 56
Quicksort 64
Big O notation revisited 70

5 hash tables 77

Hash functions 80
Use cases 84
Collisions 91
Performance 93

6 breadth-first search 101

Introduction to graphs 102
What is a graph? 104
Breadth-first search 106
Implementing the graph 111
Implementing the algorithm 113

7 trees 121

Your first tree 122
A space odyssey: Depth-first search 126
Binary trees 131
Huffman coding 133

8 balanced trees 141

A balancing act 142
Shorter trees are faster 147
AVL trees: A type of balanced tree 151
Splay trees 159
B-trees 161

9 Dijkstra's algorithm 165

Working with Dijkstra's algorithm 166
Terminology 170
Trading for a piano 172
Negative-weight edges 178
Implementation 181

10 greedy algorithms 191

The classroom scheduling problem 192
The knapsack problem 194
The set-covering problem 196

11 dynamic programming   203

The knapsack problem (revisited)   203
Knapsack problem FAQ   213
Longest common substring   220

12 k-nearest neighbors   229

Classifying oranges vs. grapefruit   229
Building a recommendations system   231
Regression   238
Introduction to machine learning   241
A high-level overview of training an ML model   244

13 where to go next   247

Linear regression   247
Inverted indexes   249
The Fourier transform   250
Parallel algorithms   251
map/reduce   252
Bloom filters and HyperLogLog   253
HTTPS and the Diffie–Hellman key exchange   255
Locality-sensitive hashing   260
Min heaps and priority queues   261
Linear programming   263
Epilogue   264

Appendix A   performance of AVL trees   265

Appendix B   NP-hard problems   267

Appendix C   answers to exercises   277

index   291

foreword

More people than ever need to learn how to program. Sure, some people literally program for their jobs (software engineers or web developers, for example). But many other jobs, not historically requiring programming, have a programming component now or will in the future. Programming also helps people understand the technological world in which they live.

Unfortunately, the benefits of programming are not equally distributed. In North American computer science (CS) programs, for example, we have a very low participation of women and some ethnic/racial groups. It's critical that we be able to expand programming and CS to a more diverse group. The solution will involve making progress on a number of fronts, including overcoming bias, training more teachers, and offering more diversified learning experiences. We need to help more people "get in."

I'm excited about Bhargava's book because it offers a new way to get into algorithms, which is a key component of effective programming. Some people will tell you that there's only one way to learn algorithms: find a dense mathematical book about algorithms, read it, and, like, understand everything. But that privileges the types of people who can learn that way, who have time to learn that way, and who need to learn that way in the first place. It also assumes that we know *why* someone wants to learn algorithms, which, let's face it, is not a fair assumption to make.

To be clear, some of my favorite CS books are exactly those kinds of mathematically oriented algorithms books. Those books work for me. They work for a lot of CS professors. But maybe that's the problem: it's too easy to assume that the way we learn is the same way that others learn. What we need are all kinds of learning resources about all kinds of CS topics, each designed for a particular audience.

Bhargava's book is intentionally designed for people who want a nonmathematical introduction to algorithms. What impresses me most here is not what Bhargava chose to include but what he chose *not* to include. You can't include everything in a book like this—that would be overwhelming and is not the point.

Bhargava's teaching expertise enables him to wring a lot of teaching out of not a lot of pages. In reading the "Dynamic Programming" chapter, for example, I was struck by the care with which Bhargava answers a lot of anticipated reader questions that other algorithm books would not answer.

I hope that this book helps you learn, whether you're trying algorithms for the first time or you've struggled to find the right resource until now. Happy Grokking!

—Daniel Zingaro, University of Toronto

preface

I first got into programming as a hobby. *Visual Basic 6 for Dummies* taught me the basics, and I kept reading books to learn more. But the subject of algorithms was impenetrable for me. I remember savoring the table of contents of my first algorithms book, thinking "I'm finally going to understand these topics!" But it was dense stuff, and I gave up after a few weeks. It wasn't until I had my first good algorithms professor that I realized how simple and elegant these ideas were.

I wrote my first illustrated blog post back in 2012. I'm a visual learner, and I really liked the illustrated style. Since then, I've written a few illustrated posts on functional programming, Git, machine learning, and concurrency. By the way, I was a mediocre writer when I started out. Explaining technical concepts is hard. Coming up with good examples takes time, and explaining a difficult concept takes time. So it's easiest to gloss over the hard stuff. I thought I was doing a pretty good job until after one of my posts got popular, a coworker came up to me and said, "I read your post, and I still don't understand this." I still had a lot to learn about writing.

Somewhere in the middle of writing these blog posts, Manning reached out to me and asked if I wanted to write an illustrated book. Well, it turns out that Manning editors know a lot about explaining technical concepts, and they taught me how to teach. I wrote this book to scratch a particular itch: I wanted to write a book that explained hard technical topics well, and I wanted an easy-to-read algorithms book.

The first edition of this book came out in 2016. Since then, more than 100,000 people have read this book. I'm delighted to see how many people have connected with the visual learning style.

With this second edition, my goal remains the same. In this book, I use illustrations and memorable examples to make concepts stick. The book is designed for readers who know how to code and want to learn more about algorithms without any math knowledge required.

The second edition fills some gaps in the first edition. I heard from a lot of readers that they wanted me to explain trees. There are now two chapters on trees in this book. I have also expanded the section on NP completeness. NP-complete is a very abstract concept, and I wanted an explanation that would make it more concrete. If you feel the same way, I hope the section on NP-complete fills that gap for you.

My writing has come a long way since that first blog post, and I hope you find this book an easy and informative read.

acknowledgments

Kudos to Manning for giving me the chance to write this book and letting me have a lot of creative freedom with it. Thanks to publisher Marjan Bace, Mike Stephens for getting me on board, and Ian Hough for being an incredibly responsive and helpful editor. Thanks also to the people on Manning's production team: Paul Wells, Debbie Holmgren, and all the others behind the scenes. In addition, I want to thank the many people who read the manuscript and offered suggestions: Daniel Zingaro, Ben Vinegar, Alexander Manning, and Maggie Wenger. Thanks to David Eisenstat, my technical reviewer, and Tony Holdroyd, the Manning technical proofreader, for catching my many errors.

Thanks to the people who helped me reach this point: Bert Bates for teaching me how to write; the folks on the Flashkit game board for teaching me how to code; the many friends who helped by reviewing chapters, giving advice, and letting me try out different explanations, including Ben Vinegar, Karl Puzon, Alex Manning, Esther Chan, Anish Bhatt, Michael Glass, Nikrad Mahdi, Charles Lee, Jared Friedman, Hema Manickavasagam, Hari Raja, Murali Gudipati, Srinivas Varadan, and others, and Gerry Brady for teaching me algorithms. Another big thank you to algorithms academics like CLRS, Knuth, and Strang. I'm truly standing on the shoulders of giants.

Dad, Mom, Priyanka, and the rest of the family: thank you for your constant support. And a big thank you to my wife Maggie, and my son Yogi. There are many adventures ahead of us, and some of them don't involve staying inside on a Friday night rewriting paragraphs.

To all the reviewers—Abhishek Koserwal, Alex Lucas, Andres Sacco, Arun Saha, Becky Huett, Cesar Augusto Orozco Manotas, Christian Sutton, Diógines Goldoni, Dirk Gómez, Ed Bacher, Eder Andres Avila Niño, Frans Oilinki, Ganesh Swaminathan, Giampiero Granatella, Glen Yu,

Greg Kreiter, Javid Asgarov, João Ferreira, Jobinesh Purushothaman, Joe Cuevas, Josh McAdams, Krishna Anipindi, Krzysztof Kamyczek, Kyrylo Kalinichenko, Lakshminarayanan AS, Laud Bentil, Matteo Battista, Mikael Byström, Nick Rakochy, Ninoslav Cerkez, Oliver Korten, Ooi Kuan San, Pablo Varela, Patrick Regan, Patrick Wanjau, Philipp Konrad, Piotr Pindel, Rajesh Mohanan, Ranjit Sahai, Rohini Uppuluri, Roman Levchenko, Sambaran Hazra, Seth MacPherson, Shankar Swamy, Srihari Sridharan, Tobias Kopf, Vivek Veerappan, William Jamir Silva, and Xiangbo Mao—your suggestions helped make this a better book.

Finally, a big thank you to all the readers who took a chance on this book, and the readers who gave me feedback in the book's forum. You really helped make this book better.

about this book

Grokking Algorithms is designed to be easy to follow. I avoid big leaps of thought. Any time a new concept is introduced, I explain it right away or tell you when I'll explain it. Core concepts are reinforced with exercises and multiple explanations so that you can check your assumptions and make sure you're following along.

I lead with examples. Instead of writing symbol soup, my goal is to make it easy for you to visualize these concepts. I also think we learn best by being able to recall something we already know, and examples make recall easier. So when you're trying to remember the difference between arrays and linked lists (explained in chapter 2), you can just think about getting seated for a movie. Also, at the risk of stating the obvious, I'm a visual learner. This book is chock-full of images.

The contents of the book are carefully curated. There's no need to write a book that covers every sorting algorithm—that's why we have Wikipedia and Khan Academy. All the algorithms I've included are practical. I've found them useful in my job as a software engineer, and they provide a good foundation for more complex topics. Happy reading!

How to use this book

The order and contents of this book have been carefully designed. If you're interested in a topic, feel free to jump ahead. Otherwise, read the chapters in order—they build on each other.

I strongly recommend executing the code for the examples yourself. I can't stress this part enough. Just type out my code samples verbatim (or download them from https://www.manning.com/books/grokking-algorithms-second-edition or https://github.com/egonschiele/grokking_algorithms) and execute them. You'll retain a lot more if you do.

I also recommend doing the exercises in this book. The exercises are short—usually just a minute or two, sometimes 5 to 10 minutes. They will help you check your thinking, so you'll know when you're off track before you've gone too far.

Who should read this book?

This book is aimed at anyone who knows the basics of coding and wants to understand algorithms. Maybe you already have a coding problem and are trying to find an algorithmic solution. Or maybe you want to understand what algorithms are useful for. Here's a short, incomplete list of people who will probably find this book useful:

- Hobbyist coders

- Coding boot camp students

- Computer science grads looking for a refresher

- Physics/math/other grads who are interested in programming

How this book is organized: A roadmap

The first three chapters of this book lay the foundations:

- *Chapter 1*—You'll learn your first practical algorithm: binary search. You also learn to analyze the speed of an algorithm using big O notation. Big O notation is used throughout the book to analyze how slow or fast an algorithm is.

- *Chapter 2*—You'll learn about two fundamental data structures: arrays and linked lists. These data structures are used throughout the book, and they're used to make more advanced data structures like hash tables (chapter 5).

- *Chapter 3*—You'll learn about recursion, a handy technique used by many algorithms (such as quicksort, covered in chapter 4).

In my experience, big O notation and recursion are challenging topics for beginners. So I've slowed down and spent extra time on these sections.

The rest of the book presents algorithms with broad applications:

- *Problem-solving techniques*—Covered in chapters 4, 10, and 11. If you come across a problem and aren't sure how to solve it efficiently, try divide and conquer (chapter 4) or dynamic programming (chapter 11). Or you may realize there's no efficient solution, and get an approximate answer using a greedy algorithm instead (chapter 10).

- *Hash tables*—Covered in chapter 5. A hash table is a very useful data structure. It contains sets of key and value pairs, like a person's name and their email address or a username and the associated password. It's hard to overstate hash tables' usefulness. When I want to solve a problem, the two plans of attack I start with are "Can I use a hash table?" and "Can I model this as a graph?"

- *Graph and tree algorithms*—Covered in chapters 6, 7, 8, and 9. Graphs are a way to model a network: a social network, or a network of roads, or neurons, or any other set of connections. Breadth-first search (chapter 6) and Dijkstra's algorithm (chapter 9) are ways to find the shortest distance between two points in a network: you can use this approach to calculate the degrees of separation between two people or the shortest route to a destination. Trees are a type of graph. They are used in databases (often B-trees), in your browser (the DOM tree), or in your file system.

- *K-nearest neighbors (KNN)*—Covered in chapter 12. This is a simple machine-learning algorithm. You can use KNN to build a recommendations system, an OCR engine, a system to predict stock values—anything that involves predicting a value ("We think Adit will rate this movie 4 stars") or classifying an object ("That letter is a Q").

- *Next steps*—Chapter 13 goes over more algorithms that would make good further reading.

About the code

All the code examples in this book use Python 3. All code in the book is presented in a fixed-width font `like this` to separate it from ordinary text. Code annotations accompany some of the listings, highlighting important concepts.

You can get executable snippets of code from the liveBook (online) version of this book at https://livebook.manning.com/book/grokking-algorithms-second-edition. The complete code for the examples in the book is available for download from the Manning website at www.manning.com and from https://github.com/egonschiele/grokking_algorithms.

I believe you learn best when you really enjoy learning—so have fun and run the code samples!

liveBook discussion forum

Purchase of *Grokking Algorithms* includes free access to liveBook, Manning's online reading platform. Using liveBook's exclusive discussion features, you can attach comments to the book globally or to specific sections or paragraphs. It's a snap to make notes for yourself, ask and answer technical questions, and receive help from the author and other users. To access the forum, go to https://livebook.manning.com/book/grokking-algorithms-second-edition. You can also learn more about Manning's forums and the rules of conduct at https://livebook.manning.com/discussion.

Manning's commitment to our readers is to provide a venue where a meaningful dialogue between individual readers and between readers and the author can take place. It is not a commitment to any specific amount of participation on the part of the author, whose contribution to the forum remains voluntary (and unpaid). We suggest you try asking the author some challenging questions lest their interest stray! The forum and the archives of previous discussions will be accessible from the publisher's website for as long as the book is in print.

about the author

Aditya Bhargava is a software engineer. He has a master's degree in computer science from the University of Chicago. He also runs a popular illustrated tech blog at adit.io.

About the technical editor

David Eisenstat is a research software engineer. He holds a PhD in Computer Science from Brown University.

introduction to algorithms | **1**

In this chapter

- You get a foundation for the rest of the book.

- You write your first search algorithm (binary search).

- You learn how to talk about the running time of an algorithm (big O notation).

An *algorithm* is a set of instructions for accomplishing a task. Every piece of code could be called an algorithm, but this book covers the more interesting bits. I chose the algorithms in this book for inclusion because they're fast, or they solve interesting problems, or both. Here are some highlights:

- Chapter 1 talks about binary search and shows how an algorithm can speed up your code. In one example, the number of steps needed goes from 4 billion down to 32!

- A GPS device uses graph algorithms (as you'll learn in chapters 6 and 9) to calculate the shortest route to your destination.

- You can use dynamic programming (discussed in chapter 11) to write an AI algorithm that plays checkers.

In each case, I'll describe the algorithm and give you an example. Then I'll talk about the running time of the algorithm in big O notation. Finally, I'll explore what other types of problems could be solved by the same algorithm.

What you'll learn about performance

The good news is that an implementation of every algorithm in this book is probably available in your favorite language, so you don't have to write each algorithm yourself! But those implementations are useless if you don't understand the tradeoffs. In this book, you'll learn to compare tradeoffs between different algorithms: Should you use merge sort or quicksort? Should you use an array or a list? Just using a different data structure can make a big difference.

What you'll learn about solving problems

You'll learn techniques for solving problems that might have been out of your grasp until now. For example:

- If you like making video games, you can write an AI system that follows the user around using graph algorithms.

- You'll learn to make a recommendations system using k-nearest neighbors.

- Some problems aren't solvable in a timely manner! The part of this book that talks about NP-complete problems shows you how to identify those problems and come up with an algorithm that gives you an approximate answer.

More generally, by the end of this book, you'll know some of the most widely applicable algorithms. You can then use your new knowledge to learn about more specific algorithms for AI, databases, and so on. Or you can take on bigger challenges at work.

What you need to know

You'll need to know basic algebra before starting this book. In particular, take this function: $f(x) = x \times 2$. What is $f(5)$? If you answered 10, you're set.

Additionally, this chapter (and this book) will be easier to follow if you're familiar with one programming language. All the examples in this book are in Python. If you don't know any programming languages and want to learn one, choose Python—it's great for beginners. If you know another language, like JavaScript, you'll be fine.

Binary search

Suppose you're searching for a person in the phone book (what an old-fashioned sentence!). Their name starts with *K*. You could start at the beginning and keep flipping pages until you get to the *K*s. But you're more likely to start at a page in the middle because you know the *K*s are going to be near the middle of the phone book.

Or suppose you're searching for a word in a dictionary, and it starts with *O*. Again, you'll start near the middle.

Now, suppose you log on to Facebook. When you do, Facebook has to verify that you have an account on the site. So it needs to search for your username in its database. Suppose your username is karlmageddon. Facebook could start from the *A*s and search for your name—but it makes more sense for it to begin somewhere in the middle.

This is a search problem. And all these cases use the same algorithm to solve the problem: *binary search*.

Binary search is an algorithm; its input is a sorted list of elements (I'll explain later why it needs to be sorted). If an element you're looking for is in that list, binary search returns the position where it's located. Otherwise, binary search returns `null`.

Here's an example.

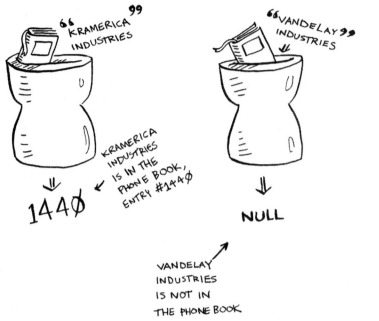

Looking for companies in a phone book with binary search

Now here's an example of how binary search works. I'm thinking of a number between 1 and 100.

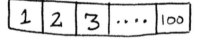

You have to try to guess my number in the fewest tries possible. With every guess, I'll tell you if your guess is too low, too high, or correct.

Suppose you start guessing like this: 1, 2, 3, 4, ... Here's how it would go.

A bad approach to number guessing

This is *simple search* (maybe *stupid search* would be a better term). With each guess, you're eliminating only one number. If my number was 99, it could take you 99 guesses to get there!

A better way to search

Here's a better technique. Start with 50.

THESE ARE ALL TOO LOW!

Too low, but you just eliminated *half* the numbers! Now you know that 1–50 are all too low. Next guess: 75.

Too high, but again you cut down half the remaining numbers! *With binary search, you guess the middle number and eliminate half the remaining numbers every time.* Next is 63 (halfway between 50 and 75).

This is binary search. You just learned your first algorithm! Here's how many numbers you can eliminate every time.

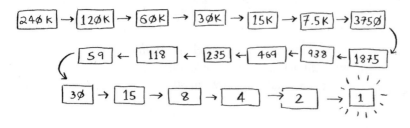

Eliminate half the numbers every time with binary search.

Whatever number I'm thinking of, you can guess in a maximum of seven guesses—because you eliminate so many numbers with every guess!

Suppose you're looking for a word in the dictionary. The dictionary has 240,000 words. *In the worst case*, how many steps do you think each search will take?

SIMPLE SEARCH: _____ STEPS

BINARY SEARCH: _____ STEPS

Simple search could take 240,000 steps if the word you're looking for is the very last one in the book. With each step of binary search, you cut the number of words in half until you're left with only one word.

So binary search will take 18 steps—a big difference! In general, for any list of *n*, binary search will take $\log_2 n$ steps to run in the worst case, whereas simple search will take *n* steps.

Logarithms

You may not remember what logarithms are, but you probably know what exponentials are. $\log_{10} 100$ is like asking, "How many 10s do we multiply together to get 100?" The answer is 2: 10×10. So $\log_{10} 100 = 2$. Logs are the inverse of exponentials.

$$10^2 = 100 \leftrightarrow \log_{10} 100 = 2$$
$$10^3 = 1000 \leftrightarrow \log_{10} 1000 = 3$$
$$2^3 = 8 \leftrightarrow \log_2 8 = 3$$
$$2^4 = 16 \leftrightarrow \log_2 16 = 4$$
$$2^5 = 32 \leftrightarrow \log_2 32 = 5$$

Logs are the inverse of exponentials.

In this book, when I talk about running time in big O notation (explained a little later), log always means $\log_2$. When you search for an element using simple search, in the worst case, you might have to look at every single element. So for a list of eight numbers, you'd have to check eight numbers at most. For binary search, you have to check log *n* elements in the worst case. For a list of eight elements, log 8 == 3, because 2^3 == 8. So for a list of eight numbers, you would have to check three numbers at most. For a list of 1,024 elements, log 1,024 = 10, because 2^{10} == 1,024. So for a list of 1,024 numbers, you'd have to check 10 numbers at most.

Note

I'll talk about log time a lot in this book, so you should understand the concept of logarithms. If you don't, Khan Academy (https://khanacademy.org) has a nice video that makes it clear.

Note

Binary search only works when your list is in sorted order. For example, the names in a phone book are sorted in alphabetical order, so you can use binary search to look for a name. What would happen if the names weren't sorted?

Let's see how to write binary search in Python. The code sample here uses arrays. If you don't know how arrays work, don't worry; they're covered in the next chapter. You just need to know that you can store a sequence of elements in a row of consecutive buckets called an array. The buckets are numbered starting with 0: the first bucket is at position 0, the second is at 1, the third is at 2, and so on.

Note

You will see me use the terms *list* and *array* interchangeably in the code. This is because in Python, arrays are called lists.

The `binary_search` function takes a sorted array and an item. If the item is in the array, the function returns its position. You'll keep track of what part of the array you have to search through. At the beginning, this is the entire array:

```
low = 0
high = len(arr) - 1
```

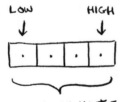

THESE ARE ALL THE
NUMBERS WE ARE
SEARCHING THROUGH

Each time, you check the middle element:

```
mid = (low + high) // 2
guess = arr[mid]
```

mid is rounded down by Python automatically if (low + high) isn't an even number.

If the guess is too low, you update `low` accordingly:

```
if guess < item:
    low = mid + 1
```

And if the guess is too high, you update `high`. Here's the full code:

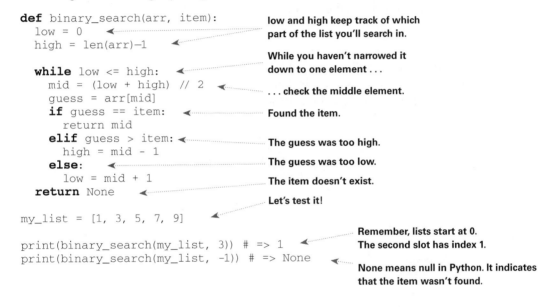

```
def binary_search(arr, item):
    low = 0
    high = len(arr)-1

    while low <= high:
        mid = (low + high) // 2
        guess = arr[mid]
        if guess == item:
            return mid
        elif guess > item:
            high = mid - 1
        else:
            low = mid + 1
    return None

my_list = [1, 3, 5, 7, 9]

print(binary_search(my_list, 3)) # => 1
print(binary_search(my_list, -1)) # => None
```

low and high keep track of which part of the list you'll search in.

While you haven't narrowed it down to one element . . .

. . . check the middle element.

Found the item.

The guess was too high.

The guess was too low.

The item doesn't exist.

Let's test it!

Remember, lists start at 0. The second slot has index 1.

None means null in Python. It indicates that the item wasn't found.

EXERCISES

1.1 Suppose you have a sorted list of 128 names, and you're searching through it using binary search. What's the maximum number of steps it would take?

1.2 Suppose you double the size of the list. What's the maximum number of steps now?

Running time

Any time I talk about an algorithm, I'll discuss its running time. Generally, you want to choose the most efficient algorithm—whether you're trying to optimize for time or space.

Back to binary search. How much time do you save by using it? Well, the first approach was to check each number, one by one. If this is a list of 100 numbers, it takes up to 100 guesses. If it's a list of 4 billion numbers, it takes up to 4 billion guesses. So the maximum number of guesses is the same as the size of the list. This is called *linear time*.

Binary search is different. If the list is 100 items long, it takes at most seven guesses. If the list is 4 billion items, it takes at most 32 guesses. Powerful, eh? Binary search runs in *logarithmic time* (or *log time*, as most people call it). Here's a table summarizing our findings today.

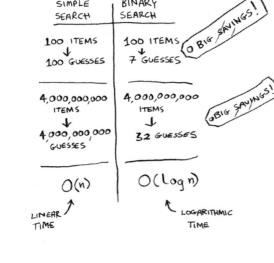

Run times for
search algorithms

Big O notation

Big O notation is special notation that tells you how fast an algorithm is. Who cares? Well, it turns out that you'll use other people's algorithms often—and when you do, it's nice to understand how fast or slow they are. In this section, I'll explain what big O notation is and give you a list of the most common running times for algorithms using it.

Algorithm running times grow at different rates

Bob is writing a search algorithm for NASA. His algorithm will kick in when a rocket is about to land on the Moon, and it will help calculate where to land.

This is an example of how the run time of two algorithms can grow at different rates. Bob is trying to decide between simple search and binary search. The algorithm needs to be both fast and correct. On one hand, binary search is faster. And Bob has only *10 seconds* to figure out where to land—otherwise, the rocket will be off course. On the other hand, simple search is easier to write, and there is less chance of bugs being introduced. And Bob *really* doesn't want bugs in the code to land a rocket! To be extra careful, Bob decides to time both algorithms with a list of 100 elements.

Let's assume it takes 1 ms to check one element. With simple search, Bob has to check 100 elements, so the search takes 100 ms to run. On the other hand, he only has to check seven elements with binary search ($\log_2 100$ is roughly 7), so that search takes 7 ms to run. But realistically, the list will have more like a billion elements. If it does, how long will simple search take? How long will binary search take? Make sure you have an answer for each question before reading on.

Running time for simple
search vs. binary search
with a list of 100 elements

Bob runs binary search with 1 billion elements, and it takes 30 ms ($\log_2 1,000,000,000$ is roughly 30). "Thirty milliseconds!" he thinks. "Binary search is about 15 times faster than simple search because simple search took 100 ms with 100 elements, and binary search took 7 ms. So simple search will take $30 \times 15 = 450$ ms, right? Way under my threshold of 10 seconds." Bob decides to go with simple search. Is that the right choice?

No. Turns out that Bob is wrong. Dead wrong. The run time for simple search with 1 billion items will be 1 billion ms, which is 11 days! The problem is that the run times for binary search and simple search *don't grow at the same rate.*

	SIMPLE SEARCH	BINARY SEARCH
100 ELEMENTS	100 ms	7 ms
10,000 ELEMENTS	10 seconds	14 ms
1,000,000,000 ELEMENTS	11 days	30 ms

Run times grow at very different speeds!

That is, as the number of items increases, binary search takes a little more time to run. But simple search takes a *lot* more time to run. So as the list of numbers gets bigger, binary search suddenly becomes a *lot* faster than simple search. Bob thought binary search was 15 times faster than simple search, but that's not correct. If the list has 1 billion items, it's more like 33 million times faster. That's why it's not enough to know how long an algorithm takes to run—you need to know how the running time increases as the list size increases. That's where big O notation comes in.

Big O notation tells you how fast an algorithm is. For example, suppose you have a list of size n. Simple search needs to check each element, so it will take n operations. The run time in big O notation is $O(n)$. Where are the seconds? There are none—big O doesn't tell you the speed in seconds. *Big O notation lets you compare the number of operations.* It tells you how fast the algorithm grows.

Binary search needs log *n* operations to check a list of size *n*. What's the running time in big O notation? It's O(log *n*). In general, big O notation is written as follows.

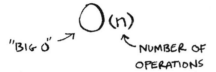

"BIG O" ➚ O (n)
↖ NUMBER OF OPERATIONS

What big O
notation looks like

This notation tells you the number of operations an algorithm will make. It's called big O notation because you put a "big O" in front of the number of operations (it sounds like a joke, but it's true!).

Now, let's look at some examples. See if you can figure out the run time for these algorithms.

Visualizing different big O run times

Here's a practical example you can follow at home with a few pieces of paper and a pencil. Suppose you have to draw a grid of 16 boxes.

Algorithm 1

One way to do it is to draw 16 boxes, one at a time. Remember, big O notation counts the number of operations. In this example, drawing one box is one operation. You have to draw 16 boxes. How many operations will it take, drawing one box at a time?

What's a good algorithm to draw this grid?

Drawing a grid one box at a time

It takes 16 steps to draw 16 boxes. What's the running time for this algorithm?

Algorithm 2

Try this algorithm instead. Fold the paper.

In this example, folding the paper once is an operation. You just made two boxes with that operation!

Fold the paper again, and again, and again.

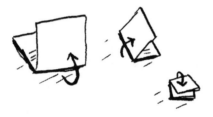

Unfold it after four folds, and you'll have a beautiful grid! Every fold doubles the number of boxes. You made 16 boxes with four operations!

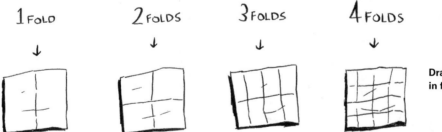

Drawing a grid in four folds

You can "draw" twice as many boxes with every fold, so you can draw 16 boxes in four steps. What's the running time for this algorithm? Come up with running times for both algorithms before moving on.

Answers: Algorithm 1 takes $O(n)$ time, and algorithm 2 takes $O(\log n)$ time.

Big O establishes a worst-case run time

Suppose you're using simple search to look for a person in the phone book. You know that simple search takes O(*n*) time to run, which means, in the worst case, you'll have to look through every single entry in your phone book. In this case, you're looking for Adit. This guy is the first entry in your phone book. So you didn't have to look at every entry—you found it on the first try. Did this algorithm take O(*n*) time? Or did it take O(1) time because you found the person on the first try?

Simple search still takes O(*n*) time. In this case, you found what you were looking for instantly. That's the best-case scenario. But we are using big O notation for *worst-case* scenario analysis. So you can say that in the *worst case*, you'll have to look at every entry in the phone book once. That's O(*n*) time. It's a reassurance—you know that simple search will never be slower than O(*n*) time.

> **Note**
>
> Along with the worst-case run time, it's also important to look at the average-case run time. Worst case versus average case is discussed in chapter 4.

Some common big O run times

Here are five big O run times that you'll encounter a lot, sorted from fastest to slowest:

- O(log *n*), also known as *log time*. Example: binary search.

- O(*n*), also known as *linear time*. Example: simple search.

- O(*n* * log *n*). Example: a fast sorting algorithm, like quicksort (coming up in chapter 4).

- O(*n*²). Example: a slow sorting algorithm, like selection sort (coming up in chapter 2).

- O(*n*!). Example: a really slow algorithm, like the traveling salesperson (coming up next!).

Suppose you're drawing a grid of 16 boxes again, and you can choose from five different algorithms to do so. If you use the first algorithm, it will take you O(log *n*) time to draw the grid. You can do 10 operations per second. With O(log *n*) time, it will take you four operations to draw a grid of 16 boxes (log 16 is 4). So it will take you 0.4 seconds to draw the grid. What if you have to draw 1,024 boxes? It will take you log 1,024 = 10 operations, or 1 second, to draw a grid of 1,024 boxes. These numbers are using the first algorithm.

The second algorithm is slower: it takes O(*n*) time. It will take 16 operations to draw 16 boxes, and it will take 1,024 operations to draw 1,024 boxes. How much time is that in seconds?

Here's how long it would take to draw a grid for the rest of the algorithms, from fastest to slowest:

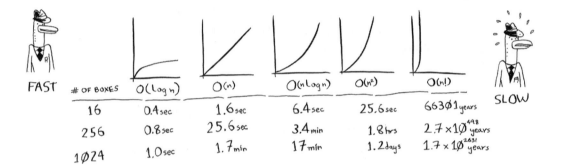

# OF BOXES	O(Log n)	O(n)	O(n Log n)	O(n²)	O(n!)
16	0.4 sec	1.6 sec	6.4 sec	25.6 sec	6630 1 years
256	0.8 sec	25.6 sec	3.4 min	1.8 hrs	2.7×10^{498} years
1024	1.0 sec	1.7 min	17 min	1.2 days	1.7×10^{2631} years

There are other run times, too, but these are the five most common.

This explanation is a simplification. In reality, you can't convert from a big O run time to a number of operations this neatly, but this is good enough for now. We'll come back to big O notation in chapter 4, after you've learned a few more algorithms. For now, the main takeaways are as follows:

- Algorithm speed isn't measured in seconds but in growth of the number of operations.

- Instead of seconds, we talk about how quickly the run time of an algorithm increases as the size of the input increases.

- Run time of algorithms is expressed in big O notation.

- O(log *n*) is faster than O(*n*), and it gets a lot faster as the list of items you're searching grows.

EXERCISES

Give the run time for each of these scenarios in terms of big O.

1.3 You have a name, and you want to find the person's phone number in the phone book.

1.4 You have a phone number, and you want to find the person's name in the phone book. (Hint: You'll have to search through the whole book!)

1.5 You want to read the numbers of every person in the phone book.

1.6 You want to read the numbers of just the *A*s. (This is a tricky one! It involves concepts that are covered more in chapter 4. Read the answer—you may be surprised!)

The traveling salesperson

You might have read that last section and thought, "There's no way I'll ever run into an algorithm that takes $O(n!)$ time." Well, let me try to prove you wrong! Here's an example of an algorithm with a really bad running time. This problem is famous in computer science because its growth is appalling and some very smart people think it can't be improved. It's called the *traveling salesperson* problem.

You have a salesperson. The salesperson has to go to five cities.

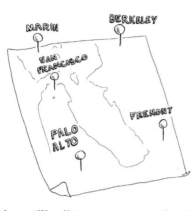

This salesperson, whom I'll call Opus, wants to hit all five cities while traveling the minimum distance. Here's one way to do that: look at every possible order in which he could travel to the cities.

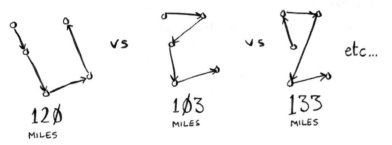

He adds up the total distance and then picks the path with the lowest distance. There are 120 permutations with five cities, so it will take 120 operations to solve the problem for five cities. For six cities, it will take 720 operations (there are 720 permutations). For seven cities, it will take 5,040 operations!

CITIES	OPERATIONS
6	720
7	5040
8	40320
...	...
15	1307674368000
...	...
30	265252859812191058636308480000000

The number
of operations
increases drastically.

In general, for *n* items, it will take *n*! (*n* factorial) operations to compute the result. So this is O(*n*!) time, or *factorial time*. It takes a lot of operations for everything except the smallest numbers. Once you're dealing with 100+ cities, it's impossible to calculate the answer in time—the Sun will collapse first.

This is a terrible algorithm! Opus should use a different one, right? But he can't. This is one of the unsolved problems in computer science. There's no fast known algorithm for it, and some smart people think it's *impossible* to have a smart algorithm for this problem. The best we can do is come up with an approximate solution; see chapter 10 for more.

Recap

- Binary search is a lot faster than simple search as your array gets bigger.

- O(log *n*) is faster than O(*n*), and it gets a lot faster once the list of items you're searching through grows.

- Algorithm speed isn't measured in seconds.

- Algorithm times are measured in terms of *growth* of an algorithm.

- Algorithm times are written in big O notation.

In this chapter

- You learn about arrays and linked lists—two of the most basic data structures. They're used absolutely everywhere. You already used arrays in chapter 1, and you'll use them in almost every chapter in this book. Arrays are a crucial topic, so pay attention! But sometimes it's better to use a linked list instead of an array. This chapter explains the pros and cons of both so you can decide which one is right for your algorithm.

- You learn your first sorting algorithm. A lot of algorithms only work if your data is sorted. Remember binary search? You can run binary search only on a sorted list of elements. This chapter teaches you selection sort. Most languages have a sorting algorithm built in, so you'll rarely need to write your own version from scratch. But selection sort is a stepping stone to quicksort, which I'll cover in chapter 4. Quicksort is an important algorithm, and it will be easier to understand if you know one sorting algorithm already.

How memory works

Imagine you go to a show and need to check your things. A chest of
drawers is available.

Each drawer can hold one element. You want to store two things, so you
ask for two drawers.

You store your two things here.

And you're ready for the show! This is basically how your computer's memory works. Your computer looks like a giant set of drawers, and each drawer has an address.

ADDRESS: fe0ffeeb

fe0ffeeb is the address of a slot in memory.

Each time you want to store an item in memory, you ask the computer for some space, and it gives you an address where you can store your item. If you want to store multiple items, there are two basic ways to do so: arrays and linked lists. I'll talk about arrays and lists next, as well as the pros and cons of each. There isn't one right way to store items for every use case, so it's important to know the differences.

Arrays and linked lists

Sometimes you need to store a list of elements in memory. Suppose you're writing an app to manage your to-dos. You'll want to store the to-dos as a list in memory.

Should you use an array or a linked list? Let's store the to-dos in an array first because it's easier to grasp. Using an array means all your tasks are stored contiguously (right next to each other) in memory.

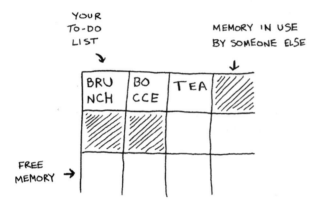

Now, suppose you want to add a fourth task. But the next drawer is taken up by someone else's stuff!

It's like going to a movie with your friends and finding a place to sit—but another friend joins you, and there's no place for them. You have to move to a new spot where you all fit. In this case, you need to ask your computer for a different chunk of memory that can fit four tasks. Then you need to move all your tasks there.

If another friend comes by, you're out of room again—and you all have to move a second time! What a pain. Similarly, adding new items to an array can be a big pain. If you're out of space and need to move to a new spot in memory every time, adding a new item will be really slow. One easy fix is to "hold seats": even if you have only three items in your task list, you can ask the computer for 10 slots, just in case. Then you can add up to 10 items to your task list without having to move. This is a good workaround, but you should be aware of a couple of downsides:

- You may not need the extra slots that you asked for, and then that memory will be wasted. You aren't using it, but no one else can use it either.

- You may add more than 10 items to your task list and have to move anyway.

So it's a good workaround, but it's not a perfect solution. Linked lists solve this problem of adding items.

Linked lists

With linked lists, your items can be anywhere in memory.

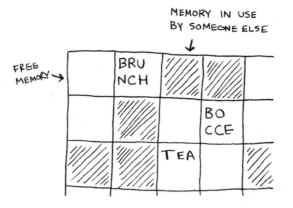

Each item stores the address of the next item in the list. A bunch of random memory addresses are linked together.

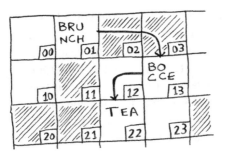

Linked memory addresses

It's like a treasure hunt. You go to the first address, and it says, "The next item can be found at address 123." So you go to address 123, and it says, "The next item can be found at address 847," and so on. Adding an item to a linked list is easy: you stick it anywhere in memory and store the address with the previous item.

With linked lists, you never have to move your items. You also avoid another problem. Let's say you go to a popular movie with five of your friends. The six of you are trying to find a place to sit, but the theater is packed. There aren't six seats together. Well, sometimes this happens with arrays. Let's say you're trying to find 10,000 slots for an array. Your memory has 10,000 slots, but it doesn't have 10,000 slots together. You can't get space for your array! A linked list is like saying, "Let's split up and watch the movie." If there's space in memory, you have space for your linked list.

If linked lists are so much better at inserts, what are arrays good for?

Arrays

Websites with top-10 lists sometimes use this tactic to get more page views. Instead of showing you the list on one page, they put one item on each page and make you click Next to get to the next item in the list. For example, Top 10 Best TV Villains won't show you the entire list on one page. Instead, you start at #10 (Newman), and you have to click Next on each page to reach #1 (Gustavo Fring). This technique gives the websites 10 whole pages on which to show you ads, but it's boring to click Next nine times to get to #1. It would be much better if the whole list was on one page and you could click each person's name for more info.

⁸/₁₀   EVIL CAT   NEXT▷

Linked lists have a similar problem. Suppose you want to read the last item in a linked list. You can't just read it because you don't know what address it's at. Instead, you have to go to item #1 to get the address for item #2. Then you have to go to item #2 to get the address for item #3. And so on, until you get to the last item. Linked lists are great if you're going to read all the items one at a time: you can read one item, follow the address to the next item, and so on. But if you're going to keep jumping around, linked lists are terrible.

Arrays are different. You know the address for every item in your array. For example, suppose your array contains five items, and you know it starts at address 00. What is the address of item #5?

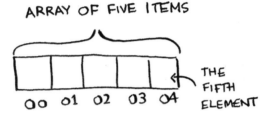

Simple math tells you: it's 04. Arrays are great if you want to read random elements because you can look up any element in your array instantly. With a linked list, the elements aren't next to each other, so you can't instantly calculate the position of the fifth element in memory—you have to go to the first element to get the address to the second element, then go to the second element to get the address of the third element, and so on until you get to the fifth element.

Terminology

The elements in an array are numbered. This numbering starts from 0, not 1. For example, in this array, 20 is at position 1.

And 10 is at position 0. This usually throws new programmers for a spin. Starting at 0 makes all kinds of array-based code easier to write, so programmers have stuck with it. Almost every programming language you use will number array elements starting at 0. You'll soon get used to it.

The position of an element is called its *index*. So instead of saying, "20 is at *position* 1," the correct terminology is, "20 is at *index* 1." I'll use *index* to mean *position* throughout this book.

Here are the run times for common operations on arrays and lists.

	ARRAYS	LISTS
READING	$O(1)$	$O(n)$
INSERTION	$O(n)$	$O(1)$

$O(n)$ = LINEAR TIME
$O(1)$ = CONSTANT TIME

Question: Why does it take O(n) time to insert an element into an array? Suppose you wanted to insert an element at the beginning of an array. How would you do it? How long would it take? Find the answers to these questions in the next section!

EXERCISE

2.1 Suppose you're building an app to keep track of your finances.

1. GROCERIES
2. MOVIE
3. SFBC
   MEMBERSHIP

Every day, you write down everything you spent money on. At the end of the month, you review your expenses and sum up how much you spent. So you have lots of inserts and a few reads. Should you use an array or a list?

Inserting into the middle of a list

Suppose you want your to-do list to work more like a calendar. Earlier, you were adding things to the end of the list.

Now, you want to add them in the order in which they should be done.

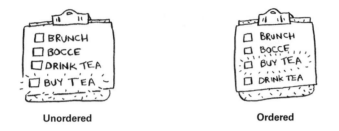

Unordered   **Ordered**

What's better if you want to insert elements in the middle: arrays or lists? With lists, it's as easy as changing what the previous element points to.

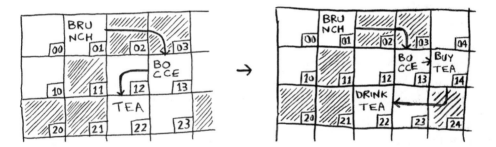

But for arrays, you have to shift all the rest of the elements down.

And if there's no space, you might have to copy everything to a new location! Lists are better if you want to insert elements into the middle.

Pointers

I have talked a lot about how each item in a linked list points to the next item in the list. But how does it do that exactly? By using pointers.

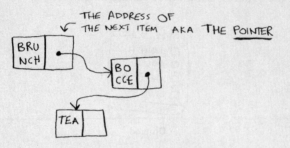

With each item in your linked list, you use a little bit of memory to store the address of the next item. This is called a *pointer*.

You will hear the word *pointers* come up sometimes, especially if you write using a lower-level language like C. So it's good to know what it means.

Deletions

What if you want to delete an element? Again, lists are better because you just need to change what the previous element points to. With arrays, everything needs to be moved up when you delete an element.

Unlike insertions, deletions will always work. Insertions can fail sometimes when there's no space left in memory. But you can always delete an element.

Here are the run times for common operations on arrays and linked lists.

	ARRAYS	LISTS
READING	O(1)	O(n)
INSERTION	O(n)	O(1)
DELETION	O(n)	O(1)

It's worth mentioning that insertions and deletions are O(1) time only if you can instantly access the element to be deleted. It's a common practice to keep track of the first and last items in a linked list, so it would take only O(1) time to delete those.

Which is used more, arrays or linked lists?

Arrays are often used because they have a lot of advantages over linked lists. First, they are better at reads. Arrays provide random access.

There are two different types of access: random access and sequential access. Sequential access means reading the elements one by one, starting with the first element. Linked lists can only do sequential access. If you want to read the 10th element of a linked list, you have to read the first nine elements and follow the links to the 10th element. Random access means you can jump directly to the 10th element. Arrays provide random access. A lot of use cases require random access, so arrays are used a lot.

Even beyond random access, though, arrays are faster because they can use caching. Maybe you are picturing reads like this, reading one item at a time.

But in reality, computers read a whole section at a time because that makes it a lot faster to go to the next item:

This is something you can do with arrays. With an array, you can read a whole section of items. But you can't do this with a linked list! You don't know where the next item is. You need to read an item, find out where the next item is, and then read the next item.

So not only do arrays give you random access, but they also provide faster sequential access!

Arrays are better for reads. What about memory efficiency? Remember earlier I said that with arrays, you typically request more space than you need, and if you don't end up using that extra memory you requested, it is wasted?

Well, in reality, there is not much wasted space like this. On the other hand, when you use a linked list, you are using extra memory per item because you need to store the address of the next item. So linked lists will take up more space if each item is pretty small. Here's the same information as an array and a linked list. You can see the linked list takes up more space.

ARRAYS

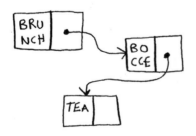

LINKED LISTS

Of course, if each item is big, then even a single slot of wasted space can be a big deal, and that extra memory you're using to store the pointers can feel pretty small by comparison.

So arrays are used more often than linked lists except in specific use cases.

EXERCISES

2.2 Suppose you're building an app for restaurants to take customer orders. Your app needs to store a list of orders. Servers keep adding orders to this list, and chefs take orders off the list and make them. It's an order queue: servers add orders to the back of the queue, and the chef takes the first order off the queue and cooks it.

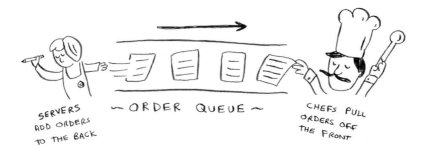

SERVERS ADD ORDERS TO THE BACK — ORDER QUEUE ~ CHEFS PULL ORDERS OFF THE FRONT

Would you use an array or a linked list to implement this queue? (Hint: Linked lists are good for inserts/deletes, and arrays are good for random access. Which one are you going to be doing here?)

2.3 Let's run a thought experiment. Suppose Facebook keeps a list of usernames. When someone tries to log in to Facebook, a search is done for their username. If their name is in the list of usernames, they can log in. People log in to Facebook pretty often, so there are a lot of searches through this list of usernames. Suppose Facebook uses binary search to search the list. Binary search needs random access—you need to be able to get to the middle of the list of usernames instantly. Knowing this, would you implement the list as an array or a linked list?

2.4 People sign up for Facebook pretty often, too. Suppose you decided to use an array to store the list of users. What are the downsides of an array for inserts? In particular, suppose you're using binary search to search for logins. What happens when you add new users to an array?

2.5 In reality, Facebook uses neither an array nor a linked list to store user information. Let's consider a hybrid data structure: an array of linked lists. You have an array with 26 slots. Each slot points to a linked list. For example, the first slot in the array points to a linked list containing all the usernames starting with *A*. The second slot points to a linked list containing all the usernames starting with *B*, and so on.

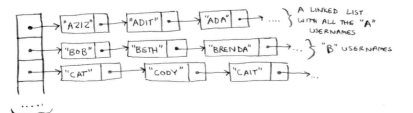

Suppose Adit B signs up for Facebook, and you want to add them to the list. You go to slot 1 in the array, go to the linked list for slot 1, and add Adit B at the end. Now, suppose you want to search for Zakhir H. You go to slot 26, which points to a linked list of all the Z names. Then you search through that list to find Zakhir H.

Compare this hybrid data structure to arrays and linked lists. Is it slower or faster than each for searching and inserting? You don't have to give big O run times, just whether the data structure would be faster or slower.

Selection sort

Let's put it all together to learn your second algorithm: selection sort. To follow this section, you need to understand arrays and big O notation.

Suppose you have a bunch of music on your computer. For each artist, you have a play count.

♫	PLAY COUNT
RADIOHEAD	156
KISHORE KUMAR	141
THE BLACK KEYS	35
NEUTRAL MILK HOTEL	94
BECK	88
THE STROKES	61
WILCO	111

You want to sort these artists from most to least played so that you can rank your favorite artists. How can you do it?

One way is to go through the list and find the most-played artist. Add that artist to a new list.

~ 🎵 ~	PLAY COUNT		🎶 SORTED 🎶	PLAY COUNT
RADIOHEAD	156		RADIOHEAD	156
KISHORE KUMAR	141			
THE BLACK KEYS	35	➡		
NEUTRAL MILK HOTEL	94			
BECK	88			
THE STROKES	61			
WILCO	111			

1. RADIOHEAD IS THE MOST PLAYED ARTIST...

2. ADD IT TO A NEW LIST

Do it again to find the next-most-played artist.

~ 🎵 ~	PLAY COUNT		🎵 SORTED 🎶	PLAY COUNT
			RADIOHEAD	156
KISHORE KUMAR	141		KISHORE KUMAR	141
THE BLACK KEYS	35	➡		
NEUTRAL MILK HOTEL	94			
BECK	88			
THE STROKES	61			
WILCO	111			

1. KISHORE KUMAR IS THE NEXT MOST-PLAYED ARTIST

2. SO IT IS THE NEXT ARTIST ADDED TO THE NEW LIST

Keep doing this, and you'll end up with a sorted list.

♫	PLAY COUNT
RADIOHEAD	156
KISHORE KUMAR	141
WILCO	111
NEUTRAL MILK HOTEL	94
BECK	88
THE STROKES	61
THE BLACK KEYS	35

Let's put on our computer science hats and see how long this will take to run. Remember that O(*n*) time means you touch every element in a list once. For example, running a simple search over the list of artists means looking at each artist once.

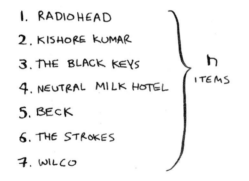

1. RADIOHEAD
2. KISHORE KUMAR
3. THE BLACK KEYS
4. NEUTRAL MILK HOTEL
5. BECK
6. THE STROKES
7. WILCO

} *n* ITEMS

To find the artist with the highest play count, you have to check each item in the list. This takes O(*n*) time, as you just saw. So you have an operation that takes O(*n*) time, and you have to do that *n* times.

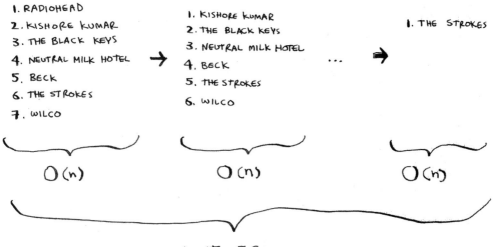

This takes O($n \times n$) time or O(n^2) time.

Sorting algorithms are very useful. Now you can sort

- Names in a phone book

- Travel dates

- Emails (newest to oldest)

Checking fewer elements each time

As you go through the operations, the number of elements you have to check keeps decreasing. Eventually, you're down to having to check just one element. So maybe you are wondering: How can the run time still be O(n^2)? That's a good question, and the answer has to do with constants in big O notation. I'll get into this more in chapter 4, but here's the gist.

You're right that you don't have to check a list of n elements each time. You check n elements, then $n - 1, n - 2, \ldots 2, 1$. On average, you check a list that has $1/2 \times n$ elements. The runtime is O($n \times 1/2 \times n$). But constants like $1/2$ are ignored in big O notation (again, see chapter 4 for the full discussion), so you just write O($n \times n$) or O(n^2).

Selection sort is a neat algorithm, but it's not very fast. Quicksort is a faster sorting algorithm that only takes O(*n* log *n*) time. It's coming up in chapter 4!

Example code listing

I didn't show you the code to sort the music list, but the following is some code that will do something very similar: sort an array from smallest to largest. Let's write a function to find the smallest element in an array:

```
def findSmallest(arr):
    smallest = arr[0]              ◄·············· Stores the smallest value
    smallest_index = 0            ◄·············· Stores the index of the smallest value
    for i in range(1, len(arr)):
      if arr[i] < smallest:
        smallest = arr[i]
        smallest_index = i
    return smallest_index
```

Now you can use this function to write selection sort:

```
def selectionSort(arr):        ◄·········· Sorts an array
    newArr = []
    copiedArr = list(arr) // copy array before mutating
    for i in range(len(copiedArr)):
        smallest = findSmallest(copiedArr)           ◄·········· Finds the smallest element in the
        newArr.append(copiedArr.pop(smallest))                  array and adds it to the new array
    return newArr

print(selectionSort([5, 3, 6, 2, 10]))
```

Recap

- Your computer's memory is like a giant set of drawers.

- When you want to store multiple elements, use an array or a linked list.

- With an array, all your elements are stored right next to each other.

- With a linked list, elements are strewn all over, and one element stores the address of the next one.

- Arrays allow fast reads.

- Linked lists allow fast inserts and deletes.

recursion | 3

In this chapter

- You learn about recursion. Recursion is a coding technique used in many algorithms. It's a building block for understanding later chapters in this book.

- You learn what a base case and a recursive case is. The divide-and-conquer strategy (chapter 4) uses this simple concept to solve hard problems.

I'm excited about this chapter because it covers *recursion*, an elegant way to solve problems. Recursion is one of my favorite topics, but it's divisive. People either love it or hate it—or hate it until they learn to love it a few years later. I personally was in that third camp. To make things easier for you, I have some advice:

- This chapter has a lot of code examples. Run the code for yourself to see how it works.

- I'll talk about recursive functions. At least once, step through a recursive function with pen and paper: something like, "Let's see, I pass 5 into `factorial`, and then I return five times passing 4 into `factorial`, which is . . . ," and so on. Walking through a function like this will teach you how a recursive function works.

This chapter also includes a lot of pseudocode. *Pseudocode* is a high-level description in code of the problem you're trying to solve. It's written like code, but it's meant to be closer to human speech.

Recursion

Suppose you're digging through your grandma's attic and come across a mysterious locked suitcase.

Grandma tells you that the key for the suitcase is probably in this other box.

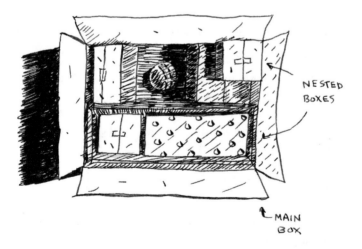

This box contains more boxes, with more boxes inside those boxes. The key is in a box somewhere. What's your algorithm to search for the key? Think of an algorithm before you read on.

Here's one approach:

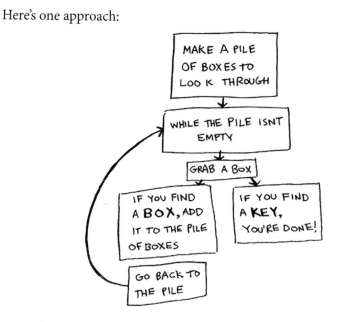

1. Make a pile of boxes to look through.

2. Grab a box and look through it.

3. If you find a box, add it to the pile to look through later.

4. If you find a key, you're done!

5. Repeat.

Here's an alternate approach:

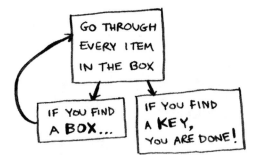

1. Look through the box.

2. If you find a box, go to step 1.

3. If you find a key, you're done!

Which approach seems easier to you? The first approach uses a `while` loop. While the pile isn't empty, grab a box and look through it. Here's some pseudocode:

```
def look_for_key(main_box):
  pile = main_box.make_a_pile_to_look_through()
  while pile is not empty:
    box = pile.grab_a_box()
    for item in box:
      if item.is_a_box():
        pile.append(item)
      elif item.is_a_key():
        print("found the key!")
```

The second way uses recursion. *Recursion* is where a function calls itself. Here's the second way in pseudocode:

```
def look_for_key(box):
  for item in box:
    if item.is_a_box():
      look_for_key(item)        ◄············ Recursion!
    elif item.is_a_key():
      print("found the key!")
```

Both approaches accomplish the same thing, but the second approach is clearer to me. Recursion is used when it makes the solution clearer. There's no performance benefit to using recursion; in fact, loops are sometimes better for performance. I like this quote by Leigh Caldwell on Stack Overflow: "Loops may achieve a performance gain for your program. Recursion may achieve a performance gain for your programmer. Choose which is more important in your situation!" (http://stackoverflow.com/a/72694/139117).

Many important algorithms use recursion, so it's important to understand the concept.

Base case and recursive case

Because a recursive function calls itself, it's easy to write a function incorrectly that ends up in an infinite loop. For example, suppose you want to write a function that prints a countdown like this:

```
> 3...2...1
```

You can write it recursively like so:

```
def countdown(i):
    print(i)
    countdown(i-1)

countdown(3)
```

Write out this code and run it. You'll notice a problem: this function will run forever!

Infinite loop

```
> 3...2...1...0...-1...-2...
```

(Press Ctrl-C to kill your script.)

When you write a recursive function, you have to tell it when to stop recursing. That's why *every recursive function has two parts: the base case and the recursive case.* The recursive case is when the function calls itself. The base case is when the function doesn't call itself again, so it doesn't go into an infinite loop.

Let's add a base case to the countdown function:

```
def countdown(i):
    print(i)
    if i <= 1:          ◀·········  Base case
        return
    else:               ◀·········  Recursive case
        countdown(i-1)

countdown(3)
```

Now the function works as expected. It goes something like this.

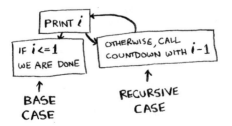

The stack

This section covers the *call stack*. The call stack is an important concept in general programming, and it's also important to understand when using recursion.

Suppose you're throwing a barbecue. You keep a to-do list for the barbecue, in the form of a stack of sticky notes.

 Remember back when we talked about arrays and lists, and you had a to-do list? You could add to-do items anywhere to the list or delete random items. The stack of sticky notes is much simpler. When you insert an item, it gets added to the top of the list. When you read an item, you only read the topmost item, and it's taken off the list. So your to-do list has only two actions: *push* (insert) and *pop* (remove and read).

PUSH
(ADD A NEW ITEM
TO THE TOP)

POP
(REMOVE THE TOPMOST
ITEM AND READ IT)

Let's see the to-do list in action.

 → →

POP A TO-DO
OFF THE STACK

IT SAYS "GET FOOD".
YOU NEED TO GET
BUNS, BURGERS AND
BAKE A CAKE

LETS PUSH THESE
TO-DOS ONTO THE STACK

This data structure is called a *stack*. The stack is a simple data structure. You've been using a stack this whole time without realizing it!

The call stack

Your computer uses a stack internally called the *call stack*. Let's see it in action. Here's a simple function:

```
def greet(name):
    print("hello, " + name + "!")
    greet2(name)
    print("getting ready to say bye...")
    bye()
```

This function greets you and then calls two other functions. Here are those two functions:

```
def greet2(name):
    print("how are you, " + name + "?")

def bye():
    print("ok bye! ")
```

Let's walk through what happens when you call a function.

Note

To keep things simple, I'm only showing the calls to greet, greet2, and bye. I'm not showing the calls to the print function.

Suppose you call greet("maggie"). First, your computer allocates a box of memory for that function call.

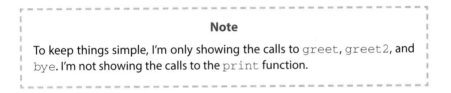

Now let's use the memory. The variable name is set to "maggie". That needs to be saved in memory.

Every time you make a function call, your computer saves the values for all the variables for that call in memory like this. Next, you print `hello, maggie!` Then you call `greet2("maggie")`. Again, your computer allocates a box of memory for this function call.

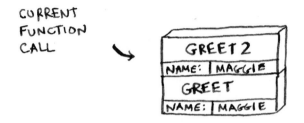

Your computer is using a stack for these boxes. The second box is added on top of the first one. You print `how are you, maggie?` Then you return from the function call. When this happens, the box on top of the stack gets popped off.

Now the topmost box on the stack is for the `greet` function, which means you returned to the `greet` function. When you called the `greet2` function, the `greet` function was *partially completed*. This is the big idea behind this section: *when you call a function from another function, the calling function is paused in a partially completed state.* All the values of the variables for that function are still stored on the call stack (i.e., in memory). Now that you're done with the `greet2` function, you're back to the `greet` function, and you pick up where you left off. First, you print `getting ready to say bye...` Then you call the `bye` function.

A box for that function is added to the top of the stack. Then you print `ok bye!` and return from the function call.

And you're back to the `greet` function. There's nothing else to be done, so you return from the `greet` function, too. This stack, used to save the variables for multiple functions, is called the *call stack*.

EXERCISE

3.1 Suppose I show you a call stack like this.

What information can you give me, just based on this call stack?

Now let's see the call stack in action with a recursive function.

The call stack with recursion

Recursive functions use the call stack, too! Let's look at this in action with the `factorial` function. `factorial(5)` is written as 5!, and it's defined like this: 5! = 5 * 4 * 3 * 2 * 1. Similarly, `factorial(3)` is 3 * 2 * 1. Here's a recursive function to calculate the factorial of a number:

```python
def fact(x):
  if x == 1:
    return 1
  else:
    return x * fact(x-1)
```

Now you can call `fact(3)`. Let's step through this call line by line and see how the stack changes. Remember, the topmost box in the stack tells you what call to `fact` you're currently on.

CODE   CALL STACK

fact(3)   FIRST CALL TO fact
                 X IS 3

if x == 1:

else:

A RECURSIVE CALL!   return x * fact(x-1)

NOW WE ARE IN   if x == 1:   THE TOPMOST FUNCTION
THE SECOND CALL   CALL IS THE CALL WE
TO fact. X IS 2   ARE CURRENTLY IN

else: NOTE: BOTH FUNCTION CALLS
               HAVE A VARIABLE NAMED X
               AND THE VALUE OF X
               IS DIFFERENT IN BOTH

return x * fact(x-1)   YOU CAN'T ACCESS
                          THIS CALL'S X
                          FROM THIS CALL
                          AND VICE VERSA

if x == 1:

WOW, WE MADE   THIS IS THE FIRST BOX
THREE CALLS TO   TO GET POPPED OFF THE
fact, BUT WE   STACK, WHICH MEANS
HAD NOT FINISHED   return 1   IT'S THE FIRST CALL WE
A SINGLE CALL UNTIL   RETURN FROM
NOW!
                                     RETURNS 1

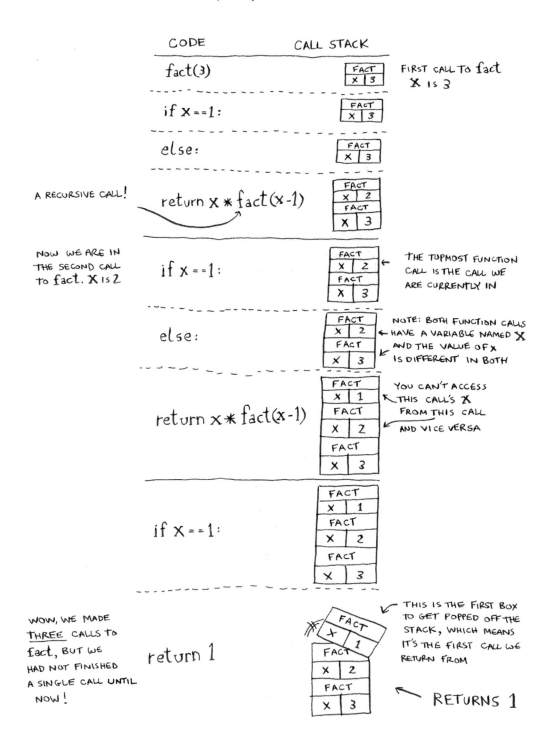

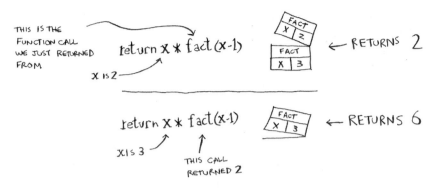

Notice that each call to `fact` has its own copy of x. You can't access a different function's copy of x.

The stack plays a big part in recursion. In the opening example, there were two approaches to finding the key. Here's the first way again.

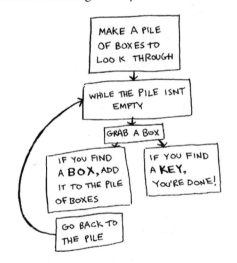

This way, you make a pile of boxes to search through, so you always know what boxes you still need to search.

But in the recursive approach, there's no pile.

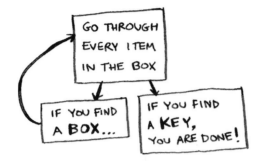

If there's no pile, how does your algorithm know what boxes you still have to look through? Here's an example.

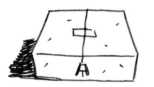

YOU LOOK THROUGH
BOX A

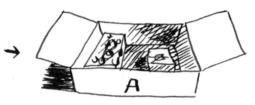

INSIDE YOU FIND
BOXES B AND C

YOU CHECK
BOX B

IT CONTAINS
BOX D

YOU CHECK
BOX D

IT IS
EMPTY

At this point, the call stack looks like this.

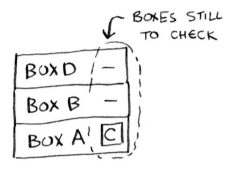

The "pile of boxes" is saved on the stack! This is a stack of half-completed function calls, each with its own half-complete list of boxes to look through. Using the stack is convenient because you don't have to keep track of a pile of boxes yourself—the stack does it for you.

Using the stack is convenient, but there's a cost: saving all that info can take up a lot of memory. Each of those function calls takes up some memory, and when your stack is too tall, that means your computer is saving information for many function calls. At that point, you have two options:

- You can rewrite your code to use a loop instead.

- You can use something called *tail recursion*. That's an advanced recursion topic that is out of the scope of this book. It's also only supported by some languages, not all.

EXERCISE

3.2 Suppose you accidentally write a recursive function that runs forever. As you saw, your computer allocates memory on the stack for each function call. What happens to the stack when your recursive function runs forever?

Recap

- Recursion is when a function calls itself.

- Every recursive function has two cases: the base case and the recursive case.

- A stack has two operations: push and pop.

- All function calls go onto the call stack.

- The call stack can get very large, which takes up a lot of memory.

quicksort | 4

In this chapter

- You learn about divide and conquer. Sometimes you'll come across a problem that can't be solved by any algorithm you've learned. When a good algorithmist encounters such a problem, they don't just give up. They have a toolbox full of techniques they use on the problem, trying to come up with a solution. Divide and conquer is the first general technique you learn.

- You learn about quicksort, an elegant sorting algorithm often used in practice. Quicksort uses divide and conquer.

You learned all about recursion in the last chapter. This chapter focuses on using your new skill to solve problems. We'll explore *divide and conquer* (D&C), a well-known recursive technique for solving problems.

This chapter really gets into the meat of algorithms. After all, an algorithm isn't very useful if it can only solve one type of problem. Instead, D&C gives you a new way to think about solving problems. D&C is another tool in your toolbox. When you get a new problem, you don't have to be stumped. Instead, you can ask, "Can I solve this if I use divide and conquer?"

At the end of the chapter, you'll learn your first major D&C algorithm: *quicksort*. Quicksort is a sorting algorithm that is much faster than selection sort (which you learned in chapter 2). It's a good example of elegant code.

Divide and conquer

D&C can take some time to grasp. So, we'll do three examples. First, I'll show you a visual example. Then I'll show a code example that is less pretty but maybe easier. Finally, we'll go through quicksort, a sorting algorithm that uses D&C.

Suppose you're a farmer with a plot of land.

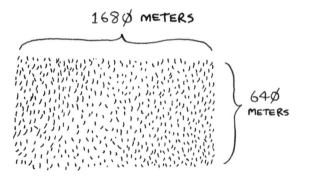

You want to divide this farm evenly into *square* plots. You want the plots to be as big as possible. So none of these will work.

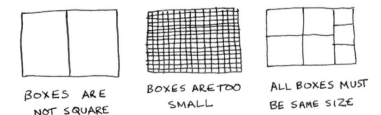

How do you figure out the largest square size you can use for a plot of land? Use the D&C strategy! D&C algorithms are recursive algorithms. There are two steps to solving a problem using D&C:

1. Figure out the base case. This should be the simplest possible case.

2. Divide or decrease your problem until it becomes the base case.

Let's use D&C to find the solution to this problem. What is the largest square size you can use?

First, figure out the base case. The easiest case would be if one side was a multiple of the other side.

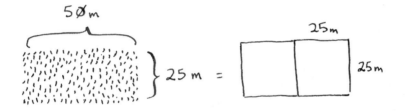

Suppose one side is 25 m and the other side is 50 m. Then the largest box you can use is 25 m × 25 m. You need two of those boxes to divide up the land.

Now you need to figure out the recursive case. This is where D&C comes in. According to D&C, with every recursive call, you have to reduce your problem. How do you reduce the problem here? Let's start by marking out the biggest boxes you can use.

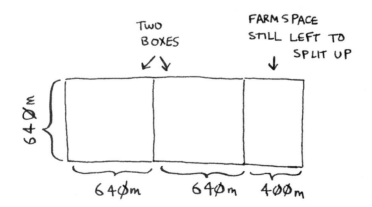

You can fit two 640 m × 640 m boxes in there, and there's some land still left to be divided. Now here comes the "Aha!" moment. There's a farm segment left to divide. *Why don't you apply the same algorithm to this segment?*

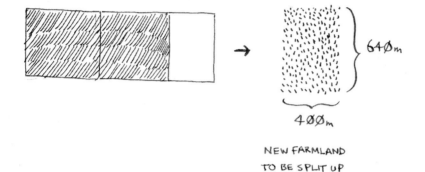

NEW FARMLAND
TO BE SPLIT UP

So you started out with a 1,680 m × 640 m farm that needed to be split up. But now you need to split up a smaller segment, 640 m × 400 m. If you *find the biggest box that will work for this size, that will be the biggest box that will work for the entire farm.* You just reduced the problem from a 1,680 m × 640 m farm to a 640 m × 400 m farm!

Euclid's algorithm

"If you find the biggest box that will work for this size, that will be the biggest box that will work for the entire farm." If it's not obvious to you why this statement is true, don't worry. It isn't obvious. Unfortunately, the proof for why it works is a little too long to include in this book, so you'll just have to believe me that it works. If you want to understand the proof, look up Euclid's algorithm for finding the greatest common denominator. The Khan Academy has a good explanation (http://mng.bz/orm2).

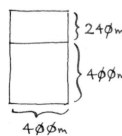

Let's apply the same algorithm again. Starting with a 640 m × 400 m farm, the biggest box you can create is 400 m× 400 m.

And that leaves you with a smaller segment, 400 m × 240 m.

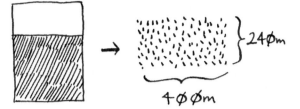

And you can draw a box on that to get an even smaller segment, 240 m × 160 m.

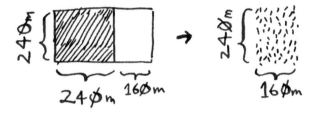

And then you draw a box on that to get an even *smaller* segment.

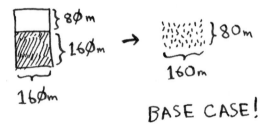

BASE CASE!

Hey, you're at the base case: 80 is a factor of 160. If you split up this segment using boxes, you don't have anything left over!

So, for the original farm, the biggest plot size you can use is 80 m × 80 m.

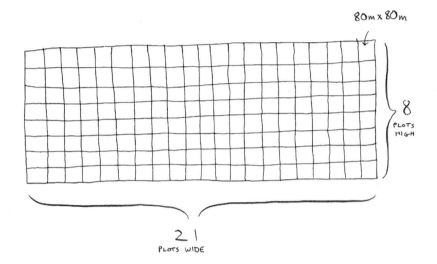

To recap, here's how D&C works:

1. Figure out a simple case as the base case.

2. Figure out how to reduce your problem and get to the base case.

D&C isn't a simple algorithm that you can apply to a problem. Instead, it's a way to think about a problem. Let's do one more example.

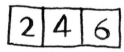

You're given an array of numbers. You have to add up all the numbers and return the total. It's pretty easy to do this with a loop:

```python
def sum(arr):
  total = 0
  for x in arr:
    total += x
  return total

print(sum([1, 2, 3, 4]))
```

But how would you do this with a recursive function?

Step 1: Figure out the base case. What's the simplest array you could get? Think about the simplest case, and then read on. If you get an array with 0 or 1 element, that's pretty easy to sum up.

BASE CASE $\begin{cases} \text{[ ]} \quad \emptyset \text{ ELEMENTS} = \text{SUM IS } \emptyset \\ \boxed{7} \quad 1 \text{ ELEMENT} = \text{SUM IS } 7 \end{cases}$

So that will be the base case.

Step 2: You need to move closer to an empty array with every recursive call. How do you reduce your problem size? Here's one way.

$$\text{Sum}\left(\boxed{2 \mid 4 \mid 6}\right) = 12$$

It's the same as this.

$$2 + \text{Sum}\left(\boxed{4 \mid 6}\right) = 2 + 10 = 12$$

In either case, the result is 12. But in the second version, you're passing a smaller array into the sum function. That is, *you decreased the size of your problem!*

Your sum function could work like this.

Here it is in action.

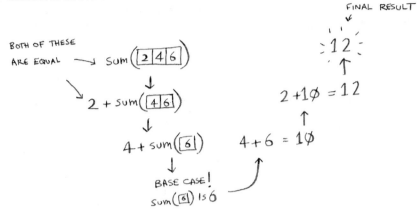

Remember, recursion keeps track of the state.

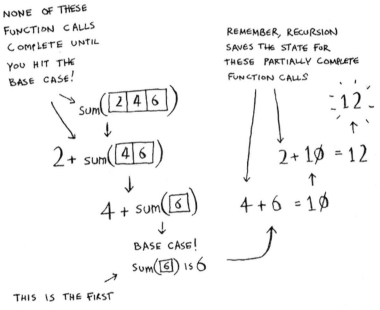

Tip

When you're writing a recursive function involving an array, the base case is often an empty array or an array with one element. If you're stuck, try that first.

Sneak peek at functional programming

"Why would I do this recursively if I can do it easily with a loop?" you may be thinking. Well, this is a sneak peek into functional programming! Functional programming languages like Haskell don't have loops, so you have to use recursion to write functions like this. If you have a good understanding of recursion, functional languages will be easier to learn. For example, here's how you'd write a sum function in Haskell:

```
sum [] = 0              ◀············· Base case
sum (x:xs) = x + (sum xs)  ◀···· Recursive case
```

Notice that it looks like you have two definitions for the function. The first definition runs when you hit the base case. The second definition runs at the recursive case. You can also write this function in Haskell using an if statement:

```
sum arr = if arr == []
              then 0
              else (head arr) + (sum (tail arr))
```

But the first definition is easier to read. Because Haskell makes heavy use of recursion, it includes all kinds of niceties like this to make recursion easy. If you like recursion or you're interested in learning a new language, check out Haskell.

EXERCISES

4.1 Write out the code for the earlier sum function.

4.2 Write a recursive function to count the number of items in a list.

4.3 Write a recursive function to find the maximum number in a list.

4.4 Remember binary search from chapter 1? It's a D&C algorithm, too. Can you come up with the base case and recursive case for binary search?

Quicksort

Quicksort is a sorting algorithm. It's much faster than selection sort and is frequently used in real life. Quicksort also uses D&C.

Let's use quicksort to sort an array. What's the simplest array that a sorting algorithm can handle (remember my tip from the previous section)? Well, some arrays don't need to be sorted at all.

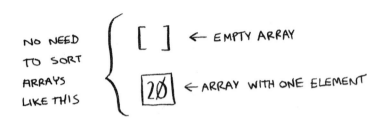

Empty arrays and arrays with just one element will be the base case. You can just return those arrays as is—there's nothing to sort:

```python
def quicksort(array):
    if len(array) < 2:
        return array
```

Let's look at bigger arrays. An array with two elements is pretty easy to sort, too.

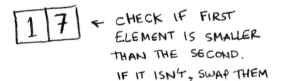

What about an array of three elements?

Remember, you're using D&C. So you want to break down this array until you're at the base case. Here's how quicksort works. First, pick an element from the array. This element is called the *pivot*.

We'll talk about how to pick a good pivot later. For now, let's say the first item in the array is the pivot.

Now find the elements smaller than the pivot and the elements larger than the pivot.

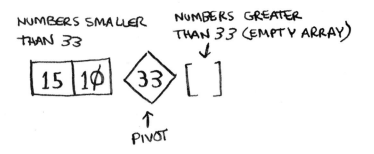

This is called *partitioning*. Now you have

- A sub-array of all the numbers less than the pivot

- The pivot

- A sub-array of all the numbers greater than the pivot

The two sub-arrays aren't sorted. They're just partitioned. But if they *were* sorted, then sorting the whole array would be pretty easy.

If the sub-arrays are sorted, then you can combine the whole thing as `left array + pivot + right array`, and you get a sorted array. In this case, it's `[10, 15] + [33] + [] = [10, 15, 33]`, which is a sorted array.

How do you sort the sub-arrays? Well, the quicksort base case already knows how to sort empty arrays (the right sub-array), and it can recursively sort arrays of two elements (the left sub-array). So if you call quicksort on the two sub-arrays and then combine the results, you get a sorted array:

```
quicksort([15, 10]) + [33] + quicksort([])
> [10, 15, 33]                          ◄········· A sorted array
```

This strategy will work with any pivot. Suppose you choose 15 as the pivot instead.

Both sub-arrays have only one element, and you know how to sort those. So now you know how to sort an array of three elements. Here are the steps:

1. Pick a pivot.

2. Partition the array into two sub-arrays: elements less than the pivot and elements greater than the pivot.

3. Call quicksort recursively on the two sub-arrays.

What about an array of four elements?

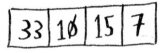

Suppose you choose 33 as the pivot again.

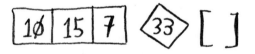

The array on the left has three elements. You already know how to sort an array of three elements: call quicksort on it recursively.

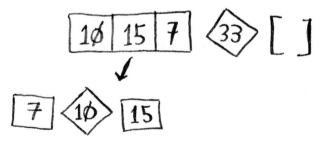

So you can sort an array of four elements. And if you can sort an array of four elements, you can sort an array of five elements. Why is that? Suppose you have this array of five elements.

Here are all the ways you can partition this array, depending on what pivot you choose.

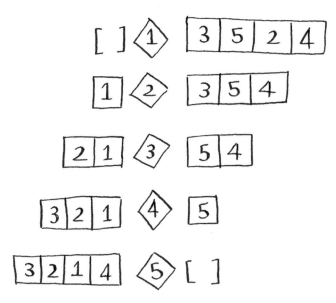

Notice that all of these sub-arrays have somewhere between zero and four elements. And you already know how to sort an array of zero to four elements using quicksort! So no matter what pivot you pick, you can call quicksort recursively on the two sub-arrays.

For example, suppose you pick 3 as the pivot. You call quicksort on the sub-arrays.

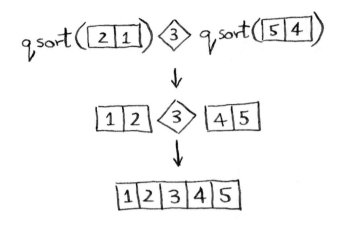

The sub-arrays get sorted, and then you combine the whole thing to get a sorted array. This works even if you choose 5 as the pivot.

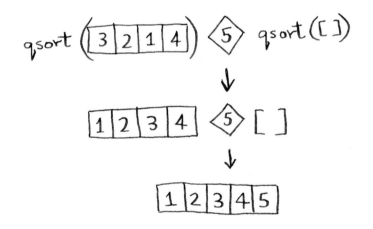

This works with any element as the pivot. So you can sort an array of five elements. Using the same logic, you can sort an array of six elements and so on.

Inductive proofs

You just got a sneak peek into *inductive proofs!* Inductive proofs are one way to prove that your algorithm works. Each inductive proof has two steps: the base case and the inductive case. Sound familiar? For example, suppose I want to prove that I can climb to the top of a ladder. In the inductive case, if my legs are on a rung, I can put my legs on the next rung. So if I'm on rung 2, I can climb to rung 3. That's the inductive case. For the base case, I'll say that my legs are on rung 1. Therefore, I can climb the entire ladder, going up one rung at a time.

You use similar reasoning for quicksort. In the base case, I showed that the algorithm works for the base case: arrays of size 0 and 1. In the inductive case, I showed that if quicksort works for an array of size 1, it will work for an array of size 2. And if it works for arrays of size 2, it will work for arrays of size 3, and so on. Then I can say that quicksort will work for all arrays of any size. I won't go deeper into inductive proofs here, but they're fun and go hand in hand with D&C.

Here's the code for quicksort:

```
def quicksort(array):
  if len(array) < 2:
    return array     ◄······· Base case: arrays with 0 or 1 element are already sorted.
  else:
    pivot = array[0]     ◄················· Recursive case
    less = [i for i in array[1:] if i <= pivot]     ◄······· Sub-array of all the elements
                                                            less than the pivot

    greater = [i for i in array[1:] if i > pivot]   ◄······· Sub-array of all the elements
                                                            greater than the pivot

    return quicksort(less) + [pivot] + quicksort(greater)

print(quicksort([10, 5, 2, 3]))
```

Big O notation revisited

Quicksort is unique because its speed depends on the pivot you choose. Before I talk about quicksort, let's look at the most common big O run times again.

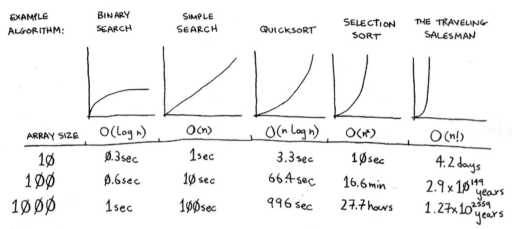

EXAMPLE ALGORITHM:	BINARY SEARCH	SIMPLE SEARCH	QUICKSORT	SELECTION SORT	THE TRAVELING SALESMAN
ARRAY SIZE	$O(\log n)$	$O(n)$	$O(n \log n)$	$O(n^2)$	$O(n!)$
10	0.3sec	1sec	3.3sec	10sec	4.2 days
100	0.6sec	10 sec	664sec	16.6min	2.9×10^{149} years
1000	1sec	100sec	996 sec	27.7hours	1.27×10^{2559} years

Estimates based on a slow computer that performs 10 operations per second

The example times in this chart are estimates if you perform 10 operations per second. These graphs aren't precise—they're just there to give you a sense of how different these run times are. In reality, your computer can do way more than 10 operations per second.

Each run time also has an example algorithm attached. Check out selection sort, which you learned in chapter 2. It's $O(n^2)$. That's a pretty slow algorithm.

There's another sorting algorithm called *merge sort*, which is $O(n \log n)$. Much faster! Quicksort is a tricky case. In the worst case, quicksort takes $O(n^2)$ time.

It's as slow as selection sort! But that's the worst case. In the average case, quicksort takes $O(n \log n)$ time. So you might be wondering:

What do *worst case* and *average case* mean here?

If quicksort is $O(n \log n)$ on average, but merge sort is $O(n \log n)$ always, why not use merge sort? Isn't it faster?

Merge sort vs. quicksort

Suppose you have this simple function to print every item in a list:

```
def print_items(myList):
    for item in myList:
        print(item)
```

This function goes through every item in the list and prints it out. Because it loops over the whole list once, this function runs in O(*n*) time. Now, suppose you change this function so it sleeps for 1 second before it prints out an item:

```
from time import sleep
def print_items2(myList):
    for item in myList:
        sleep(1)
        print(item)
```

Before it prints out an item, it will pause for 1 second. Suppose you print a list of five items using both functions.

2 | 4 | 6 | 8 | 10

print_items: 2 4 6 8 10

print_items 2: \<sleep\> 2 \<sleep\> 4 \<sleep\> 6 \<sleep\> 8 \<sleep\> 10

Both functions loop through the list once, so they're both O(*n*) time. Which one do you think will be faster in practice? I think `print_items` will be much faster because it doesn't pause for 1 second before printing an item. So even though both functions are the same speed in big O notation, `print_items` is faster in practice. When you write big O notation like O(*n*), it really means this.

c is some fixed amount of time that your algorithm takes. It's called the *constant*. For example, it might be `10 milliseconds * n` for `print_items` versus `1 second * n` for `print_items2`.

You usually ignore that constant because if two algorithms have different big O times, the constant doesn't matter. Take binary search and simple search, for example. Suppose both algorithms had these constants.

$$\frac{10ms * n}{\text{SIMPLE SEARCH}} \qquad \frac{1sec * \log n}{\text{BINARY SEARCH}}$$

You might say, "Wow! Simple search has a constant of 10 ms, but binary search has a constant of 1 second. Simple search is way faster!" Now suppose you're searching a list of 4 billion elements. Here are the times.

$$\text{SIMPLE SEARCH} \quad \Big| \quad 10ms * 4 \text{ BILLION} = 463 \text{ days}$$
$$\text{BINARY SEARCH} \quad \Big| \quad 1sec * 32 \quad = \quad 32 \text{ seconds}$$

We're using 32 for binary search because binary search runs in log time and log(4 billion) equals 32. As you can see, binary search is still way faster. That constant didn't make a difference at all.

But sometimes the constant *can* make a difference. Quicksort versus merge sort is one example. Often, given the way quicksort and merge sort are implemented, if they're both $O(n \log n)$ time, quicksort is faster. And quicksort is faster in practice because it hits the average case way more often than the worst case.

So now you're wondering: What's the average case versus the worst case?

Average case vs. worst case

The performance of quicksort heavily depends on the pivot you choose. Suppose you always choose the first element as the pivot. And you call quicksort with an array that is *already sorted*. Quicksort doesn't check to see whether the input array is already sorted. So it will still try to sort it.

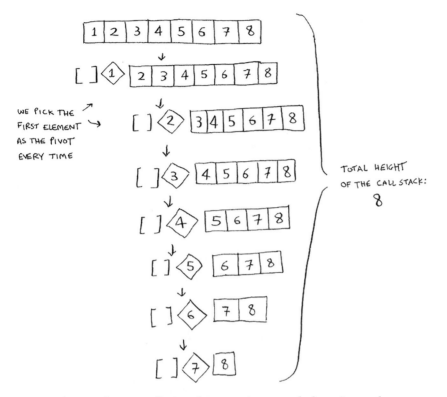

WE PICK THE
FIRST ELEMENT
AS THE PIVOT
EVERY TIME

TOTAL HEIGHT
OF THE CALL STACK:
8

Notice that you're not splitting the array into two halves. Instead, one of the sub-arrays is always empty. So the call stack is really long. Now, instead, suppose you always picked the middle element as the pivot. Look at the call stack now.

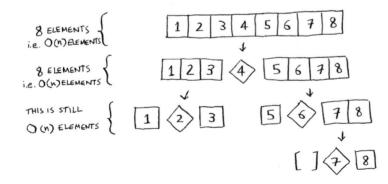

8 ELEMENTS
i.e. O(n) ELEMENTS

8 ELEMENTS
i.e. O(n) ELEMENTS

THIS IS STILL
O(n) ELEMENTS

It's so short! Because you divide the array in half every time, you don't need to make as many recursive calls. You hit the base case sooner, and the call stack is much shorter.

The first example you saw is the worst-case scenario, and the second example is the best-case scenario. In the worst case, the stack size is O(n). In the best case, the stack size is O(log n). Read on to find out how this affects the worst and average case running times.

Look at the first level in the stack. You pick one element as the pivot, and the rest of the elements are divided into sub-arrays. You touch all eight elements in the array. So this first operation takes O(n) time. You touched all eight elements on this level of the call stack. But actually, you touch O(n) elements on every level of the call stack.

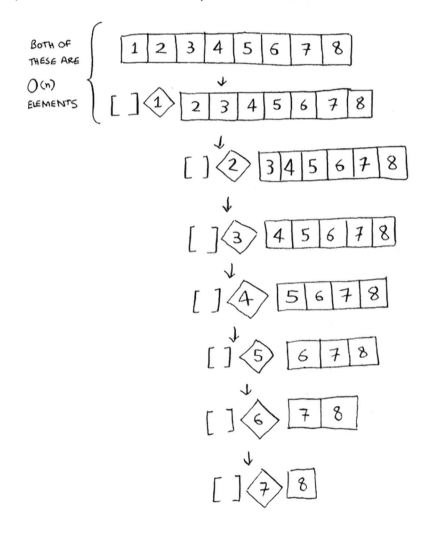

Even if you partition the array differently, you're still touching O(*n*) elements every time.

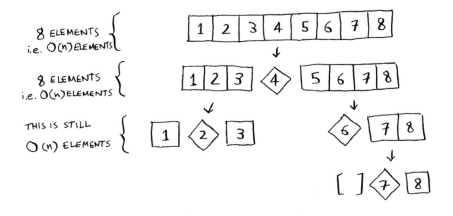

In this example, there are O(log *n*) levels (the technical way to say that is, "The height of the call stack is O(log *n*)"). And each level takes O(*n*) time. The entire algorithm will take O(*n*) * O(log *n*) = O(*n* log *n*) time. This is the best-case scenario.

In the worst case, there are O(*n*) levels, so the algorithm will take O(*n*) * O(*n*) = O(*n*²) time.

Well, guess what? I'm here to tell you that the best case is also the average case. *If you always choose a random element in the array as the pivot*, quicksort will complete in O(*n* log *n*) time on average. (There's one exception: if all the elements in your array are the same, you will always hit the worst-case run time without some additional logic.)

Quicksort is one of the fastest sorting algorithms out there, and it's a very good example of D&C.

EXERCISES

How long would each of these operations take in big O notation?

4.5 Printing the value of each element in an array.

4.6 Doubling the value of each element in an array.

4.7 Doubling the value of just the first element in an array.

4.8 Creating a multiplication table with all the elements in the array. So if your array is [2, 3, 7, 8, 10], you first multiply every element by 2, then multiply every element by 3, then by 7, and so on.

	2	3	7	8	10
2	4	6	14	16	20
3	6	9	21	24	30
7	14	21	49	56	70
8	16	24	56	64	80
10	20	30	70	80	100

Recap

- D&C works by breaking a problem down into smaller and smaller pieces. If you're using D&C on a list, the base case is probably an empty array or an array with one element.

- If you're implementing quicksort, choose a random element as the pivot. The average run time of quicksort is O(*n* log *n*)!

- Given two algorithms with the same big O running time, one can be consistently faster than the other. That's why quicksort is faster than merge sort.

- The constant almost never matters for simple search versus binary search because O(log *n*) is so much faster than O(*n*) when your list gets big.

hash tables | 5

In this chapter

- You learn about hash tables, one of the most useful data structures. Hash tables have many uses; this chapter covers the common use cases.

- You learn about the internals of hash tables: implementation, collisions, and hash functions. These properties will help you understand how to analyze a hash table's performance.

Suppose you work at a grocery store. When a customer buys produce, you have to look up the price in a book. If the book is unalphabetized, it can take you a long time to look through every single line for *apple*. You'd be doing simple search from chapter 1, where you have to look at every line. Do you remember how long that would take? O(*n*) time. If the book is alphabetized, you could run binary search to find the price of an apple. That would only take O(log *n*) time.

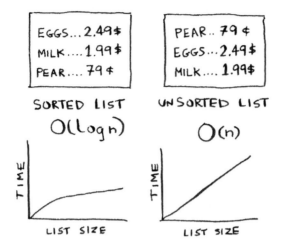

As a reminder, there's a big difference between O(*n*) and O(log *n*) time! Suppose you could look through 10 lines of the book per second. Here's how long simple search and binary search would take you.

# OF ITEMS IN THE BOOK	O(n)	O(log n)
100	10 sec	1 sec ← YOU NEED TO CHECK $\log_2 100$ = 7 LINES
1000	1.66 min	1 sec ← NEED TO CHECK $\log_2 1000$ = 10 LINES
10000	16.6 min	2 sec ← $\log_2 10000$ = 14 LINES = 2 sec

You already know that binary search is darn fast. But as a cashier, looking things up in a book is a pain, even if the book is sorted. You can feel the customer steaming up as you search for items in the book. What you really need is a buddy who has all the names and prices memorized. Then you don't need to look up anything: you ask her, and she tells you the answer instantly.

Your buddy Maggie can give you the price in O(1) time for any item, no matter how big the book is. She's even faster than binary search.

# OF ITEMS IN THE BOOK	SIMPLE SEARCH $O(n)$	BINARY SEARCH $O(\log n)$	MAGGIE $O(1)$
100	10 sec	1 sec	INSTANT
1000	1.6 min	1 sec	INSTANT
10000	16.6 min	2 sec	INSTANT

What a wonderful person! How do you get a "Maggie"?

Let's put on our data structure hats. You know two data structures so far: arrays and lists (I won't talk about stacks because you can't really "search" for something in a stack). You could implement this book as an array.

$$(\text{EGGS}, 2.49) \quad (\text{MILK}, 1.49) \quad (\text{PEAR}, 0.79)$$

Each item in the array is really two items: one is the name of a kind of produce, and the other is the price. If you sort this array by name, you can run binary search on it to find the price of an item. So you can find items in O(log *n*) time. But you want to find items in O(1) time. That is, you want to make a "Maggie." That's where hash functions come in.

Hash functions

A hash function is a function where you put in a string (*string* here means any kind of data—a sequence of bytes), and you get back a number.

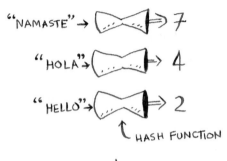

...etc...

In technical terminology, we'd say that a hash function "maps strings to numbers." You might think there's no discernable pattern to what number you get out when you put a string in. But there are some requirements for a hash function:

- It needs to be consistent. For example, suppose you put in "apple" and get back "3." Every time you put in "apple," you should get "3" back. Without this, your hash table won't work.

- It should map different words to different numbers. For example, a hash function is no good if it always returns "1" for any word you put in. In the best case, every different word should map to a different number.

So a hash function maps strings to numbers. What is that good for? Well, you can use it to make your "Maggie"!

Start with an empty array:

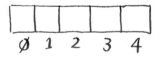

You'll store all of your prices in this array. Let's add the price of an apple. Feed "apple" into the hash function.

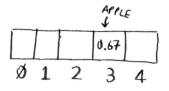

The hash function outputs "3." So let's store the price of an apple at index 3 in the array.

APPLE
↓

			0.67	
Ø	1	2	3	4

Let's add milk. Feed "milk" into the hash function.

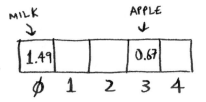

The hash function says "0." Let's store the price of milk at index 0.

MILK   APPLE
↓   ↓

1.49			0.67	
Ø	1	2	3	4

Keep going, and eventually the whole array will be full of prices.

1.49	0.79	2.49	0.67	1.49

Now you ask, "Hey, what's the price of an avocado?" You don't need to search for it in the array. Just feed "avocado" into the hash function.

"AVOCADO" → ▷ 4

It tells you that the price is stored at index 4. And sure enough, there it is.

AVOCADO = 1.49

1.49	0.79	2.49	0.67	1.49

The hash function tells you exactly where the price is stored, so you don't have to search at all! This works because

- The hash function consistently maps a name to the same index. Every time you put in "avocado," you'll get the same number back. So you can use it the first time to find where to store the price of an avocado, and then you can use it to find where you stored that price.

- The hash function maps different strings to different indexes. "Avocado" maps to index 4. "Milk" maps to index 0. Everything maps to a different slot in the array where you can store its price.

- The hash function knows how big your array is and only returns valid indexes. So if your array is five items, the hash function doesn't return 100—that wouldn't be a valid index in the array.

You just built a "Maggie"! Put a hash function and an array together, and you get a data structure called a *hash table*. A hash table is the first data structure you'll learn that has some extra logic behind it. Arrays and lists map straight to memory, but hash tables are smarter. They use a hash function to intelligently figure out where to store elements.

Hash tables are probably the most useful complex data structure you'll learn. They're also known as hash maps, maps, dictionaries, and associative arrays. And hash tables are fast! Remember our discussion of arrays and linked lists back in chapter 2? You can get an item from an array instantly. And hash tables use an array to store the data, so they're equally fast.

What's the catch?

The hash function we just saw is called a *perfect hash function*. It deftly maps each grocery item to its very own slot in the array:

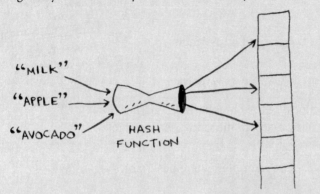

Look at them all snug in their own slots. In reality, you probably won't get a perfect one-to-one mapping like this. Your items will need to share a room. Some grocery items will map to the same slot, while other slots will go empty.

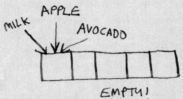

There's a section on collisions coming up that discusses this. For now, just know that while hash tables are very useful, they rarely map items to slots so perfectly.

By the way, this kind of one-to-one mapping is called an *injective function*. Use that to impress your friends!

You'll probably never have to implement hash tables yourself. Any good language will have an implementation for hash tables. Python has hash tables; they're called *dictionaries*. You can make a new hash table using empty braces:

```
>>> book = {}
```

AN EMPTY
HASH TABLE

book is a new hash table. Let's add some prices to book:

```
>>> book["apple"] = 0.67
>>> book["milk"] = 1.49
>>> book["avocado"] = 1.49
>>> print(book)
{'avocado': 1.49, 'apple': 0.67, 'milk': 1.49}
```

◄········· **An apple costs 67 cents.**
◄········· **Milk costs $1.49.**

A HASH TABLE OF
PRODUCE PRICES

Pretty easy! Now let's ask for the price of an avocado:

```
>>> print(book["avocado"])
1.49
```

◄········· **The price of an avocado**

A hash table has keys and values. In the book hash, the names of produce are the keys, and their prices are the values. A hash table maps keys to values.

In the next section, you'll see some examples where hash tables are really useful.

EXERCISES

It's important for hash functions to consistently return the same output for the same input. If they don't, you won't be able to find your item after you put it in the hash table!

Which of these hash functions are consistent?

5.1 f(x) = 1   ◄········· **Returns 1 for all input**

5.2 f(x) = random.random()   ◄····· **Returns a random number every time**

5.3 f(x) = next_empty_slot()   ◄········· **Returns the index of the next empty slot in the hash table**

5.4 f(x) = len(x)   ◄····· **Uses the length of the string as the index**

Use cases

Hash tables are used everywhere. This section will show you a few use cases.

Using hash tables for lookups

Your phone has a handy phonebook built in. Each name has a phone number associated with it.

BADE MAMA → 581 660 9820

ALEX MANNING → 484 234 4680

JANE MARIN → 415 567 3579

Suppose you want to build a phone book like this. You're mapping people's names to phone numbers. Your phone book needs to have this functionality:

- Add a person's name and the phone number associated with that person.

- Enter a person's name and get the phone number associated with that name.

This is a perfect use case for hash tables! Hash tables are great when you want to

- Create a mapping from one thing to another thing

- Look something up

Building a phone book is pretty easy. First, make a new hash table:

```
>>> phone_book = {}
```

Let's add the phone numbers of some people to this phone book:

```
>>> phone_book["jenny"] = "8675309"
>>> phone_book["emergency"] = "911"
```

That's all there is to it! Now suppose you want to find Jenny's phone number. Just pass the key in to the hash:

```
>>> print(phone_book["jenny"])
8675309       ◄┈┈┈┈┈┈┈┈┈┈┈   Jenny's phone number
```

A HASH TABLE AS A PHONE BOOK

Imagine if you had to do this using an array instead. How would you do it? Hash tables make it easy to model a relationship from one item to another.

Hash tables are used for lookups on a much larger scale. For example, suppose you go to a website like http://adit.io. Your computer has to translate adit.io to an IP address.

ADIT.IO → 173.255.248.55

For any website you go to, the address has to be translated to an IP address.

GOOGLE.COM → 74.125.239.133

FACEBOOK.COM → 173.252.120.6

SCRIBD.COM → 23.235.47.175

Wow, mapping a web address to an IP address? Sounds like a perfect use case for hash tables! This process is called *DNS resolution*. Hash tables are one way to provide this functionality. Your computer has a *DNS cache*, which stores this mapping for websites you have recently visited, and a good way to build a DNS cache is to use a hash table.

Preventing duplicate entries

Suppose you're running a voting booth. Naturally, every person can vote just once. How do you make sure they haven't voted before? When someone comes in to vote, you ask for their full name. Then you check it against the list of people who have voted.

If their name is on the list, this person has already voted—kick them out! Otherwise, you add their name to the list and let them vote. Now suppose a lot of people have come in to vote, and the list of people who have voted is really long.

Each time someone new comes in to vote, you have to scan this giant list to see if they've already voted. But there's a better way: use a hash!

First, make a hash to keep track of the people who have voted:

```
>>> voted = {}
```

When someone new comes in to vote, check if they're already in the hash:

```
>>> value = "tom" in voted
```

`value` is now `True` if "tom" is in the hash table. Otherwise, it is `False`. You can use this to check whether someone has already voted!

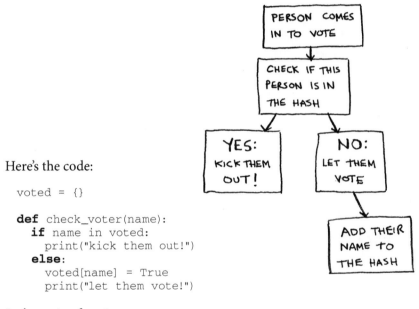

Here's the code:

```
voted = {}

def check_voter(name):
  if name in voted:
    print("kick them out!")
  else:
    voted[name] = True
    print("let them vote!")
```

Let's test it a few times:

```
>>> check_voter("tom")
let them vote!
>>> check_voter("mike")
let them vote!
>>> check_voter("mike")
kick them out!
```

The first time Tom goes in, the hash table will print, "let them vote!" Then Mike goes in, and it prints, "let them vote!" Then Mike tries to go a second time, and it prints, "kick them out!"

Remember, if you were storing these names in a list of people who have voted, this function would eventually become really slow, because it would have to run a simple search over the entire list. But you're storing their names in a hash table instead, and a hash table instantly tells you whether this person's name is in the hash table or not. Checking for duplicates is very fast with a hash table.

Using hash tables as a cache

One final use case: caching. If you work on a website, you may have heard of caching before as a good thing to do. Here's the idea. Suppose you visit https://facebook.com:

1. You make a request to Facebook's server.

2. The server thinks for a second and comes up with the web page to send you.

3. You get a web page.

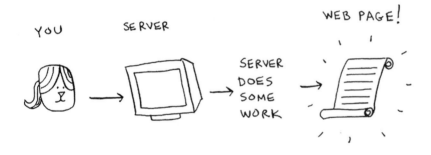

For example, on Facebook, the server may be collecting all of your friends' activity to show you. It takes a couple of seconds to collect all that activity and show it to you. As a user, that couple of seconds can feel like a long time. You might think, "Why is Facebook being so slow?" On the other hand, Facebook's servers have to serve millions of people, and that couple of seconds adds up. Facebook's servers are really working hard to serve all of those websites. Is there a way to have Facebook's servers do less work?

Suppose you have a niece who keeps asking you about planets. "How far is Mars from Earth?" "How far is the Moon?" "How far is Jupiter?" Each time, you have to do a Google search and give her an answer. It takes a couple of minutes. Now, suppose she always asked, "How far is the Moon?" Pretty soon, you'd memorize that the Moon is 238,900 miles away. You wouldn't have to look it up on Google; you'd just remember and answer. This is how caching works: websites remember the data instead of recalculating it.

If you're logged in to Facebook, all the content you see is tailored just for you. Each time you go to https://facebook.com, its servers have to think about what content you're interested in. But if you're not logged in to Facebook, you see the login page. Everyone sees the same login page. Facebook is asked the same thing over and over: "Give me the home page when I'm logged out." So it stops making the server do work to figure out what the home page looks like. Instead, it memorizes what the home page looks like and sends it to you.

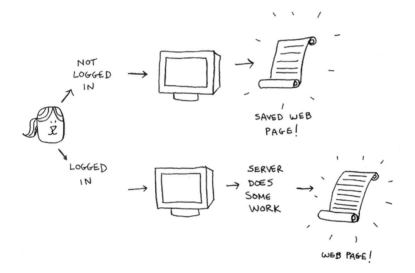

This is called *caching*. It has two advantages:

- You get the web page a lot faster, just like when you memorized the distance from Earth to the Moon. The next time your niece asks you, you won't have to Google it. You can answer instantly.

- Facebook has to do less work.

Caching is a common way to make things faster. All big websites use caching. And that data is cached in a hash!

Facebook isn't just caching the home page. It's also caching the About page, the Contact page, the Terms and Conditions page, and a lot more. So it needs a mapping from page URL to page data.

facebook.com/about → DATA FOR THE ABOUT PAGE

facebook.com → DATA FOR THE HOME PAGE

When you visit a page on Facebook, it first checks whether the page is stored in the hash.

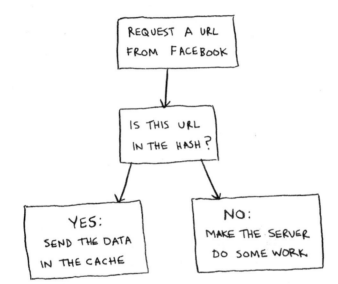

Here it is in pseudocode:

```
cache = {}

def get_page(url):
    if url in cache:
        return cache[url]          ◀┈┈┈┈  Returns cached data
    else:
        data = get_data_from_server(url)
        cache[url] = data          ◀┈┈┈┈  Saves this data in your cache first
        return data
```

Here, you make the server do work only if the URL isn't in the cache. Before you return the data, though, you save it in the cache. The next time someone requests this URL, you can send the data from the cache instead of making the server do the work.

Recap

To recap, hashes are good for

- Modeling relationships from one thing to another thing

- Filtering out duplicates

- Caching/memoizing data instead of making your server do work

Collisions

Like I said earlier, most languages have hash tables. You don't need to know how to write your own. So, I won't talk about the internals of hash tables too much. But you still care about performance! To understand the performance of hash tables, you first need to understand what collisions are. The next two sections cover collisions and performance.

First, I've been telling you a white lie. I told you that a hash function always maps different keys to different slots in the array.

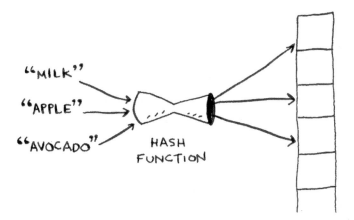

In reality, it's almost impossible to write a hash function that does this. Let's take a simple example. Suppose your array contains 26 slots.

And your hash function is really simple: it assigns a spot in the array alphabetically.

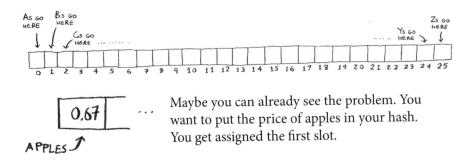

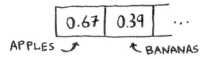

APPLES ↗

Maybe you can already see the problem. You want to put the price of apples in your hash. You get assigned the first slot.

Then you want to put the price of bananas in the hash. You get assigned the second slot.

| 0.67 | 0.39 | ... |

APPLES ↗   ↖ BANANAS

Everything is going so well! But now you want to put the price of avocados in your hash. You get assigned the first slot again.

| 0.67 | 0.39 | ... |

APPLES? ↗   ↖ BANANAS
AVOCADOS?

Oh no! Apples have that slot already! What to do? This is called a *collision*: two keys have been assigned the same slot. This is a problem. If you store the price of avocados at that slot, you'll overwrite the price of apples. Then the next time someone asks for the price of apples, they will get the price of avocados instead! Collisions are bad, and you need to work around them. There are many different ways to deal with collisions. The simplest one is this: if multiple keys map to the same slot, start a linked list at that slot.

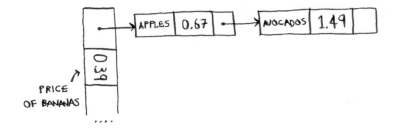

In this example, both "apples" and "avocados" map to the same slot. So you start a linked list at that slot. If you need to know the price of bananas, it's still quick. If you need to know the price of apples, it's a little slower. You have to search through this linked list to find "apples." If the linked list is small, no big deal—you have to search through three or four elements. But suppose you work at a grocery store where you only sell produce that starts with the letter *A*.

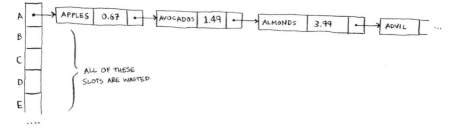

Hey, wait a minute! The entire hash table is totally empty except for one slot. And that slot has a giant linked list! Every single element in this hash table is in the linked list. That's as bad as putting everything in a linked list to begin with. It's going to slow down your hash table.

There are two lessons here:

- *Your hash function is really important.* Your hash function mapped all the keys to a single slot. Ideally, your hash function would map keys evenly all over the hash.

- If those linked lists get long, it slows down your hash table a lot. But they won't get long if you *use a good hash function*!

Hash functions are important. A good hash function will give you very few collisions. So how do you pick a good hash function? That's coming up in the next section!

Performance

You started this chapter at the grocery store. You wanted to build something that would give you the prices for produce *instantly*. Well, hash tables are really fast.

In the average case, hash tables take O(1) for everything. O(1) is called *constant time*. You haven't seen constant time before. It doesn't mean

	AVERAGE CASE	WORST CASE
SEARCH	O(1)	O(n)
INSERT	O(1)	O(n)
DELETE	O(1)	O(n)

PERFORMANCE OF HASH TABLES

instant. It means the time taken will stay the same, regardless of how big the hash table is. For example, you know that simple search takes linear time.

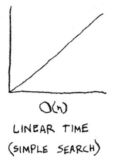

O(n)

LINEAR TIME
(SIMPLE SEARCH)

Binary search is faster—it takes log time.

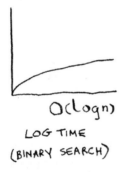

O(Logn)

LOG TIME
(BINARY SEARCH)

Looking something up in a hash table takes constant time.

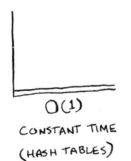

O(1)

CONSTANT TIME
(HASH TABLES)

See how it's a flat line? That means it doesn't matter whether your hash table has 1 element or 1 billion elements—getting something out of a hash table will take the same amount of time. Actually, you've seen constant time before. Getting an item out of an array takes constant time. It doesn't matter how big your array is; it takes the same amount of time to get an element. In the average case, hash tables are really fast.

In the worst case, a hash table takes O(*n*)—linear time—for everything, which is really slow. Let's compare hash tables to arrays and lists.

	HASH TABLES (AVERAGE)	HASH TABLES (WORST)	ARRAYS	LINKED LISTS
SEARCH	O(1)	O(n)	O(1)	O(n)
INSERT	O(1)	O(n)	O(n)	O(1)
DELETE	O(1)	O(n)	O(n)	O(1)

Look at the average case for hash tables. Hash tables are as fast as arrays at searching (getting a value at an index). And they're as fast as linked lists at inserts and deletes. It's the best of both worlds! But in the worst case, hash tables are slow at all of those. So it's important that you don't hit worst-case performance with hash tables. And to do that, you need to avoid collisions. To avoid collisions, you need

- A low load factor

- A good hash function

Note

Before you start this next section, know that it isn't required reading. I'm going to talk about how to implement a hash table, but you'll never have to do that yourself. Whatever programming language you use will have an implementation of hash tables built in. You can use the built-in hash table and assume it will have good performance. The next section gives you a peek under the hood.

Load factor

The load factor of a hash table is easy to calculate.

Hash tables use an array for storage, so you count the number of occupied slots in an array. For example, this hash table has a load factor of 2/5, or 0.4.

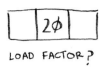

NUMBER OF ITEMS IN HASH TABLE
―――――――――
TOTAL NUMBER OF SLOTS

OCCUPIED

LOAD FACTOR = 2/5

What's the load factor of this hash table?

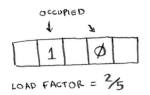

LOAD FACTOR ?

If you said 1/3, you're right. Load factor measures how full your hash table is.

Suppose you need to store the price of 100 produce items in your hash table, and your hash table has 100 slots. In the best case, each item will get its own slot.

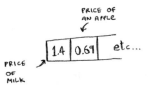

PRICE OF AN APPLE

PRICE OF MILK

This hash table has a load factor of 1. What if your hash table has only 50 slots? Then it has a load factor of 2. There's no way each item will get its own slot because there aren't enough slots! Having a load factor greater than 1 means you have more items than slots in your array. Once the load factor starts to grow, you need to add more slots to your hash table. This is called *resizing*. For example, suppose you have this hash table that is getting pretty full.

You need to resize this hash table. First, you create a new array that's bigger. The rule of thumb is to make an array twice the size of the original.

Now you need to reinsert all of those items into this new hash table using the hash function.

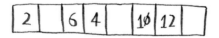

This new table has a load factor of 3/8. Much better! With a lower load factor, you'll have fewer collisions, and your table will perform better. A good rule of thumb is to resize when your load factor is greater than 0.7.

You might be thinking, "This resizing business takes a lot of time!" And you're right. Resizing is expensive, and you don't want to resize too often. But averaged out, hash tables take O(1) even with resizing.

A good hash function

A good hash function distributes values in the array evenly.

A bad hash function groups values together and produces a lot of collisions.

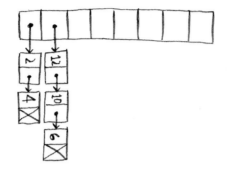

What is a good hash function? That's something you'll never have to worry about—smart folks sit in dark rooms and worry about that. If you're really curious, look up CityHash. That's what Google's Abseil library uses. Abseil is an open source C++ library based on internal Google code. It provides all kinds of general-purpose C++ functions. Abseil is a building block for Google's code, so if it uses CityHash, you can be sure that CityHash is pretty good. You could use that as your hash function.

EXERCISES

It's important for hash functions to have a good distribution. They should map items as broadly as possible. The worst case is a hash function that maps all items to the same slot in the hash table.

Suppose you have these four hash functions that work with strings:

1. Return "1" for all input.

2. Use the length of the string as the index.

3. Use the first character of the string as the index. So, all strings starting with *a* are hashed together, and so on.

4. Map every letter to a prime number: a = 2, b = 3, c = 5, d = 7, e = 11, and so on. For a string, the hash function is the sum of all the characters modulo the size of the hash. For example, if your hash size is 10, and the string is "bag," the index is $(3 + 2 + 17) \% 10 = 22 \% 10 = 2$.

For each of these examples, which hash functions would provide a good distribution? Assume a hash table size of 10 slots.

5.5 A phonebook where the keys are names and values are phone numbers. The names are as follows: Esther, Ben, Bob, and Dan.

5.6 A mapping from battery size to power. The sizes are A, AA, AAA, and AAAA.

5.7 A mapping from book titles to authors. The titles are *Maus*, *Fun Home*, and *Watchmen*.

Recap

- You'll almost never have to implement a hash table yourself. The programming language you use should provide an implementation for you. You can use Python's hash tables and assume that you'll get the average-case performance: constant time.

- Hash tables are a powerful data structure because they're so fast and they let you model data in a different way. You might soon find that you're using them all the time.

- You can make a hash table by combining a hash function with an array.

- Collisions are bad. You need a hash function that minimizes collisions.

- Hash tables have really fast search, insert, and delete.

- Hash tables are good for modeling relationships from one item to another item.

- Once your load factor is greater than 0.7, it's time to resize your hash table.

- Hash tables are used for caching data (for example, with a web server).

- Hash tables are great for catching duplicates.

breadth-first search | 6

In this chapter

- You learn how to model a network using a new, abstract data structure: graphs.

- You learn breadth-first search, an algorithm you can run on graphs to answer questions like, "What's the shortest path to go to X?"

- You learn about directed versus undirected graphs.

- You learn topological sort, a different kind of sorting algorithm that exposes dependencies between nodes.

This chapter introduces graphs. First, I'll talk about what graphs are (they don't involve an X or Y axis). Then I'll show you your first graph algorithm. It's called *breadth-first search* (BFS).

Breadth-first search allows you to find the shortest distance between two things. But shortest distance can mean a lot of things! You can use breadth-first search to

- Write a spellchecker (fewest edits from your misspelling to a real word—for example, READED → READER is one edit).

- Find the doctor closest to you in your network.

- Build a search engine crawler.

Graph algorithms are some of the most useful algorithms I know. Make sure you read the next few chapters carefully—these are algorithms you'll be able to apply again and again.

Introduction to graphs

Suppose you're in San Francisco, and you want to go from Twin Peaks to the Golden Gate Bridge. You want to get there by bus, with the minimum number of transfers. Here are your options.

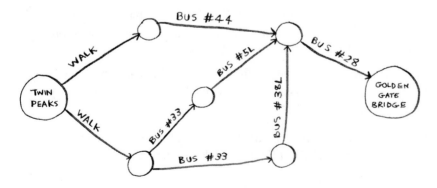

What's your algorithm to find the path with the fewest steps?

Well, can you get there in one step? Here are all the places you can get to in one step.

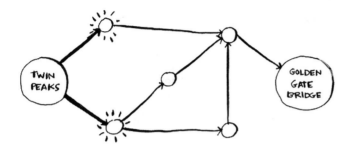

The bridge isn't highlighted; you can't get there in one step. Can you get there in two steps?

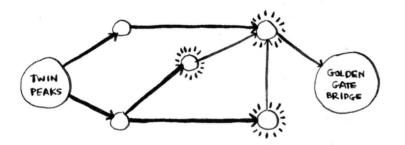

Again, the bridge isn't there, so you can't get to the bridge in two steps. What about three steps?

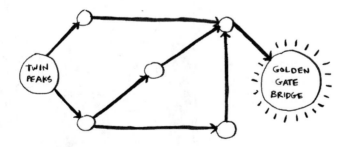

Aha! Now the Golden Gate Bridge shows up. So it takes three steps to get from Twin Peaks to the bridge using this route.

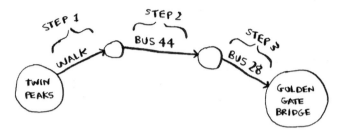

There are other routes that will get you to the bridge, too, but they're longer (four steps). The algorithm found that the shortest route to the bridge is three steps long. This type of problem is called a *shortest-path problem*. You're always trying to find the shortest something. It could be the shortest route to your friend's house. Or maybe you're browsing the web. Without you knowing it, the network is looking for the shortest path between your computer and a website's server. The algorithm to solve a shortest-path problem is called *breadth-first search*.

There are two steps to figuring out how to get from Twin Peaks to the Golden Gate Bridge:

1.   Model the problem as a graph.

2.   Solve the problem using breadth-first search.

Next I'll cover what graphs are. Then I'll go into breadth-first search in more detail.

What is a graph?

A graph models a set of connections. For example, suppose you and your friends are playing poker, and you want to model who owes whom money. Here's how you could say, "Alex owes Rama money."

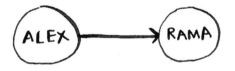

The full graph could look something like this.

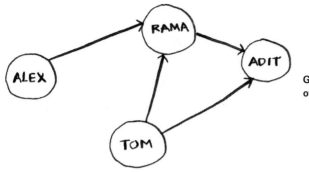

Graph of people who owe other people poker money

Alex owes Rama money, Tom owes Adit money, and so on. Each graph is made up of *nodes* and *edges*.

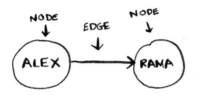

That's all there is to it! Graphs are made up of nodes and edges. A node can be directly connected to many other nodes. Those nodes are called *in-neighbors* or *out-neighbors*.

Since Alex is pointing to Rama, Alex is Rama's *in-neighbor,* and Rama is Alex's *out-neighbor.* This terminology can be confusing, so here's a diagram to help.

In the graph, Adit isn't Alex's in-neighbor or out-neighbor because they aren't directly connected. But Adit is Rama's and Tom's out-neighbor.

Graphs are a way to model how different things are connected to one another. Now let's see breadth-first search in action.

Breadth-first search

We looked at a search algorithm in chapter 1: binary search. Breadth-first search is a different kind of search algorithm: one that runs on graphs. It can help answer two types of questions:

- Question type 1: Is there a path from node A to node B?

- Question type 2: What is the shortest path from node A to node B?

You already saw breadth-first search once when you calculated the shortest route from Twin Peaks to the Golden Gate Bridge. That was a question of type 2: "What is the shortest path?" Now let's look at the algorithm in more detail. You'll ask a question of type 1: "Is there a path?"

Suppose you're the proud owner of a mango farm. You're looking for a mango seller who can sell your mangoes. Are you connected to a mango seller on Facebook? Well, you can search through your friends.

This search is pretty straightforward. First, make a list of friends to search.

Now, go to each person in the list and check whether that person sells mangoes.

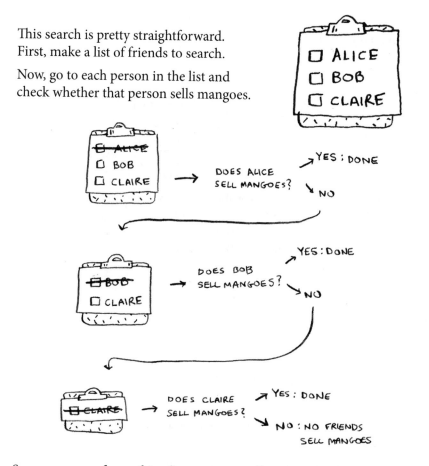

Suppose none of your friends are mango sellers. Now you have to search through your friends' friends.

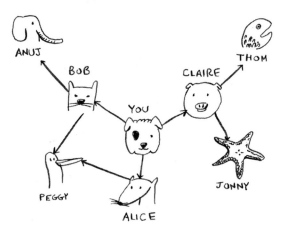

Each time you search for someone from the list, add all of their friends
to the list.

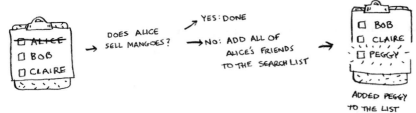

ADDED PEGGY
TO THE LIST

This way, you not only search your friends, but you search their friends,
too. Remember, the goal is to find one mango seller in your network.
So if Alice isn't a mango seller, you add her friends to the list, too. That
means you'll eventually search her friends—and then their friends, and
so on. With this algorithm, you'll search your entire network until you
come across a mango seller. This algorithm is breadth-first search.

Finding the shortest path

As a recap, these are the two questions that breadth-first search can
answer for you:

- Question type 1: Is there a path from node A to node B? (Is there a
  mango seller in your network?)

- Question type 2: What is the shortest path from node A to node B?
  (Who is the closest mango seller?)

You saw how to answer question 1; now let's try to answer question 2. Can
you find the closest mango seller? For example, your friends are first-
degree connections, and their friends are second-degree connections.

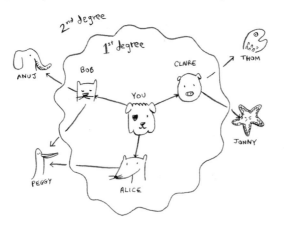

You'd prefer a first-degree connection to a second-degree connection, a second-degree connection to a third-degree connection, and so on. So you shouldn't search any second-degree connections before you make sure you don't have a first-degree connection who is a mango seller. Well, breadth-first search already does this! The way breadth-first search works is that the search radiates out from the starting point. So you'll check first-degree connections before second-degree connections. Pop quiz: Who will be checked first, Claire or Anuj? Answer: Claire is a first-degree connection, and Anuj is a second-degree connection, so Claire will be checked before Anuj.

Another way to see this is that first-degree connections are added to the search list before second-degree connections.

You just go down the list and check people to see whether each one is a mango seller. The first-degree connections will be searched before the second-degree connections, so you'll find the mango seller closest to you. Breadth-first search not only finds a path from A to B; it also finds the shortest path.

Notice that this only works if you search people in the same order in which they're added. That is, if Claire was added to the list before Anuj, Claire needs to be searched before Anuj. What happens if you search Anuj before Claire, and they're both mango sellers? Well, Anuj is a second-degree contact, and Claire is a first-degree contact. You end up with a mango seller who isn't the closest to you in your network. So you need to search people in the order that they're added. There's a data structure for this: it's called *a queue*.

Queues

A queue works exactly like it does in real life. Suppose you and your friend are queueing up at the bus stop. If you're before them in the queue, you get on the bus first. A queue works the same way. Queues are similar to stacks. You can't access random elements in the queue. Instead, there are only two operations, *enqueue* and *dequeue*.

ENQUEUE
ADD AN ITEM TO
THE QUEUE

DEQUEUE
TAKE AN ITEM OFF
THE QUEUE

If you enqueue two items to the list, the first item you added will be dequeued before the second item. You can use this for your search list! People who are added to the list first will be dequeued and searched first.

The queue is called a *FIFO* data structure: first in, first out. In contrast, a stack is a *LIFO* data structure: last in, first out.

FIFO
(FIRST IN, FIRST OUT)

LIFO
(LAST IN, FIRST OUT)

Now that you know how a queue works, let's implement breadth-first search!

EXERCISES

Run the breadth-first search algorithm on each of these graphs to find the solution.

6.1 Find the length of the shortest path from start to finish.

6.2 Find the length of the shortest path from "cab" to "bat."

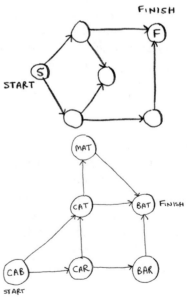

Implementing the graph

First, you need to implement the graph in code.
A graph consists of several nodes.

And each node is connected to other nodes.
How do you express a relationship like "you →
bob"? Luckily, you know a data structure that
lets you express relationships: *a hash table!*

Remember, a hash table allows you to map a key
to a value. In this case, you want to map a node
to all of its out-neighbors.

Here's how you'd write it in Python:

```
graph = {}
graph["you"] = ["alice", "bob", "claire"]
```

Notice that "you" is mapped to an array. So `graph["you"]` will give
you an array of all the out-neighbors of "you." Remember that the out-
neighbors are the nodes that the "you" node points to.

A graph is just a bunch of nodes and edges, so this is all you need to
have a graph in Python. What about a bigger graph like this one?

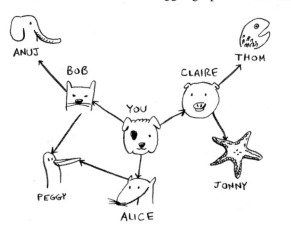

Here it is as Python code:

```
graph = {}
graph["you"] = ["alice", "bob", "claire"]
graph["bob"] = ["anuj", "peggy"]
graph["alice"] = ["peggy"]
graph["claire"] = ["thom", "jonny"]
graph["anuj"] = []
graph["peggy"] = []
graph["thom"] = []
graph["jonny"] = []
```

Pop quiz: Does it matter what order you add the key/value pairs in?
Does it matter if you write

```
graph["claire"] = ["thom", "jonny"]
graph["anuj"] = []
```

instead of

```
graph["anuj"] = []
graph["claire"] = ["thom", "jonny"]
```

Think back to the previous chapter. Answer: It doesn't matter. Hash
tables have no ordering, so it doesn't matter what order you add key/
value pairs in.

Anuj, Peggy, Thom, and Jonny don't have any out-neighbors. They have
in-neighbors since they have arrows pointing to them, but no arrows
point from them to someone else. This is called a *directed graph*: the
relationship is only one way. An undirected graph doesn't have any
arrows. For example, both of these graphs are equal.

**DIRECTED   UNDIRECTED
GRAPH   GRAPH**

If you have an undirected graph, you can forget the terms in-neighbor
and out-neighbor and use the simpler term *neighbor*.

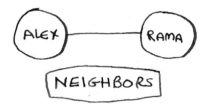

NEIGHBORS

Implementing the algorithm

To recap, here's how the implementation will work.

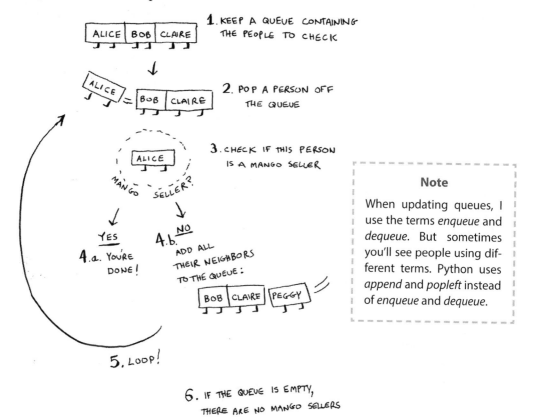

1. KEEP A QUEUE CONTAINING THE PEOPLE TO CHECK

2. POP A PERSON OFF THE QUEUE

3. CHECK IF THIS PERSON IS A MANGO SELLER

MANGO SELLER?

YES

4.a. YOU'RE DONE!

4.b. NO

ADD ALL THEIR NEIGHBORS TO THE QUEUE:

5. LOOP!

6. IF THE QUEUE IS EMPTY, THERE ARE NO MANGO SELLERS IN YOUR NETWORK

> **Note**
>
> When updating queues, I use the terms *enqueue* and *dequeue*. But sometimes you'll see people using different terms. Python uses *append* and *popleft* instead of *enqueue* and *dequeue*.

Make a queue to start. In Python, you use the double-ended queue (`deque`) function for this:

```
from collections import deque
search_queue = deque()            ◄········  Creates a new queue
search_queue += graph["you"]      ◄········  Adds all of your out-neighbors to the search queue
```

Remember, `graph["you"]` will give you a list of all your out-neighbors, like `["alice"`, `"bob"`, `"claire"]`. Those all get added to the search queue.

☐ ALICE
☐ BOB
☐ CLAIRE

Let's see the rest:

```
while search_queue:          ◄········· While the queue isn't empty . . .
    person = search_queue.popleft()   ◄·········  . . . grabs the first person off the queue.
    if person_is_seller(person):   ◄·········  Checks whether the person is a mango seller
        print(person + " is a mango seller!")   ◄·········  Yes, they're a mango seller.
        return True
    else:
        search_queue += graph[person]   ◄·········  No, they aren't. Add all of
return False   ◄·········                            this person's friends to the
                        If you reached here, no      search queue.
                        one in the queue is a
                        mango seller.
```

One final thing: you still need a `person_is_seller` function to tell you
when someone is a mango seller. Here's one:

```
def person_is_seller(name):
    return name[-1] == 'm'
```

This function checks whether the person's name ends with the letter *m*.
If it does, they're a mango seller. Kind of a silly way to do it, but it'll do
for this example. Now let's see the breadth-first search in action.

...etc...

And so on. The algorithm will keep going until either a mango seller is found or the queue becomes empty, in which case there is no mango seller.

Alice and Bob share a friend, Peggy. So Peggy will be added to the queue twice: once when you add Alice's friends and again when you add Bob's friends. You'll end up with two Peggys in the search queue.

But you only need to check Peggy once to see whether she's a mango seller. If you check her twice, you're doing unnecessary, extra work. So once you search a person, you should mark that person as searched and not search them again.

If you don't do this, you could also end up in an infinite loop. Suppose the mango seller graph looked like this.

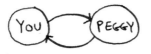

To start, the search queue contains all of your out-neighbors.

Now you check Peggy. She isn't a mango seller, so you add all her out-neighbors to the search queue.

Next, you check yourself. You're not a mango seller, so you add all your out-neighbors to the search queue.

And so on. This will be an infinite loop because the search queue will keep going from you to Peggy.

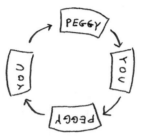

Before checking a person, it's important to make sure they haven't been checked already. To do that, you'll keep a set of people you've already checked.

Here's the final code for breadth-first search, taking that into account:

```
def search(name):
    search_queue = deque()
    search_queue += graph[name]
    searched = set()                          This set is how you keep track of which
    while search_queue:                       people you've searched before.
        person = search_queue.popleft()
        if not person in searched:            Only search this person if you
            if person_is_seller(person):      haven't already searched them.
                print(person + " is a mango seller!")
                return True
            else:
                search_queue += graph[person]
                searched.add(person)          Marks this person
    return False                              as searched

search("you")
```

Try running this code yourself. Maybe try changing the `person_is_seller` function to something more meaningful and see if it prints what you expect.

Running time

If you search your entire network for a mango seller, that means you'll follow each edge (remember, an edge is the arrow or connection from one person to another). So the running time is at least O(number of edges).

You also keep a queue of every person to search. Adding one person to the queue takes constant time: O(1). Doing this for every person will take O(number of people) total. Breadth-first search takes O(number of people + number of edges), and it's more commonly written as O(V+E) (V for number of vertices; E for number of edges).

EXERCISES

Here's a small graph of my morning routine.

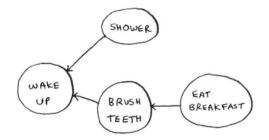

It tells you that I can't eat breakfast until I've brushed my teeth. So "eat breakfast" *depends on* "brush teeth."

On the other hand, showering doesn't depend on brushing my teeth because I can shower before I brush my teeth. From this graph, you can make a list of the order in which I need to do my morning routine:

1.   Wake up.

2.   Shower.

3.   Brush teeth.

4.   Eat breakfast.

Note that "shower" can be moved around, so this list is also valid:

1. Wake up.

2. Brush teeth.

3. Shower.

4. Eat breakfast.

6.3 For these three lists, mark whether each one is valid or invalid.

A.

1. WAKE UP

2. SHOWER

3. EAT BREAKFAST

4. BRUSH TEETH

B.

1. WAKE UP

2. BRUSH TEETH

3. EAT BREAKFAST

4. SHOWER

C.

1. SHOWER

2. WAKE UP

3. BRUSH TEETH

4. EAT BREAKFAST

6.4 Here's a larger graph. Make a valid list for this graph.

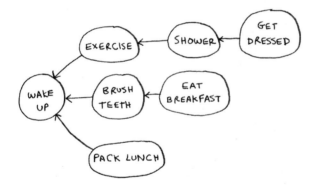

You could say that this list is sorted, in a way. If task A depends on task B, task A shows up later in the list. This is called a *topological sort*, and it's a way to make an ordered list out of a graph. Suppose you're planning a wedding and have a large graph full of tasks to do, and you're not sure where to start. You could *topologically sort* the graph and get a list of tasks to do in order.

Suppose you have a family tree.

This is a graph, because you have nodes (the people) and edges.

The edges point to the nodes' parents. But all the edges go down—it wouldn't make sense for a family tree to have an edge pointing back up! That would be meaningless—your dad can't be your grandfather's dad!

This is called a *tree*. A tree is a special type of graph where no edges ever point back.

6.5 Which of the following graphs are also trees?

A.   B.   C.

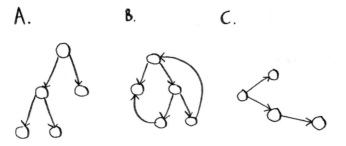

Recap

- Breadth-first search tells you if there's a path from A to B.

- If there's a path, breadth-first search will find the shortest path.

- If you have a problem like "find the shortest X," try modeling your problem as a graph and use breadth-first search to solve it.

- A directed graph has arrows, and the relationship follows the direction of the arrow (rama → adit means "rama owes adit money").

- Undirected graphs don't have arrows, and the relationship goes both ways (ross — rachel means "ross dated rachel and rachel dated ross").

- Queues are FIFO (first in, first out).

- Stacks are LIFO (last in, first out).

- You need to check people in the order they were added to the search list, so the search list needs to be a queue. Otherwise, you won't get the shortest path.

- Once you check someone, make sure you don't check them again. Otherwise, you might end up in an infinite loop.

In this chapter

- You learn what a tree is and the difference between trees and graphs.

- You get comfortable with running an algorithm over a tree.

- You learn depth-first search and see the difference between depth-first search and breadth-first search.

- You learn Huffman coding, a compression algorithm that makes use of trees.

What do compression algorithms and database storage have in common? There is often a tree underneath doing all the hard work. Trees are a subset of graphs. They are worth covering separately as there are many specialized types of trees. For example, Huffman coding, a compression algorithm you will learn in this chapter, uses binary trees.

Most databases use a balanced tree like a B-tree, which you will learn about in the next chapter. There are so many types of trees out there. These two chapters will give you the vocabulary and concepts you need to understand them.

Your first tree

Trees are a type of graph. We will have a more thorough definition later. First, let's learn some terminology and look at an example.

Just like graphs, trees are made of nodes and edges.

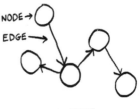

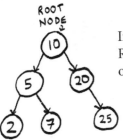

In this book, we will work with rooted trees. Rooted trees have one node that leads to all the other nodes.

We will work exclusively with rooted trees, so when I say *tree* in this chapter, I mean a rooted tree. Nodes can have children, and child nodes can have a parent.

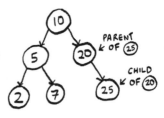

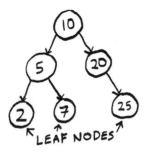

In a tree, nodes have at most one parent. The only node with no parents is the root. Nodes with no children are called leaf nodes.

If you understand root, leaf, parent, and child, you are ready to read on!

File Directories

Since a tree is a type of a graph, we can run a graph algorithm on it. In chapter 6, we learned breadth-first search, an algorithm for finding the shortest path in a graph. We are going to use breadth-first search on a tree. If you are not comfortable with breadth-first search, check out chapter 6.

A file directory is a tree that all of us interact with every day. Suppose I have this file directory.

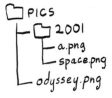

I want to print the name of every file in the pics directory, including all its subdirectories. Here, there is only one subdirectory, 2001. We can use breadth-first search to do this! First, let me show you what this file directory looks like as a tree.

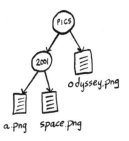

Since this file directory is a tree, we can run a graph algorithm on it. Earlier, we used breadth-first search as a search algorithm. But search isn't the only thing it's good for. Breadth-first search is a traversal algorithm. That means it is an algorithm that visits every node in a tree—that is, it traverses or walks the tree. That's exactly what we need! We need an algorithm that will go to every file in this tree and print out its name. We will use breadth-first search to list all the files in a directory. The algorithm will also go into subdirectories, find files in there, and print out their names. My logic will be as follows:

1. Visit every node in the tree.

2. If this node is a file, print out its name.

3. If the node is a folder, add it to a queue of folders to search for files.

The code follows. It is very similar to the mango seller code from
chapter 6:

```python
from os import listdir
from os.path import isfile, join
from collections import deque

def printnames(start_dir):
    search_queue = deque()
    search_queue.append(start_dir)
    while search_queue:
        dir = search_queue.popleft()
        for file in sorted(listdir(dir)):
            fullpath = join(dir, file)
            if isfile(fullpath):
                print(file)
            else:
                search_queue.append(fullpath)

printnames("pics")
```

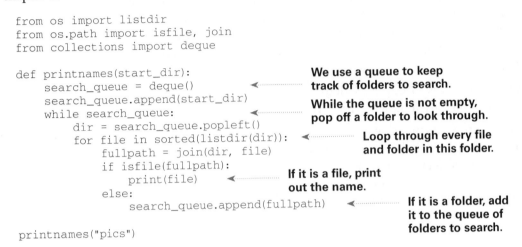

We use a queue to keep
track of folders to search.

While the queue is not empty,
pop off a folder to look through.

Loop through every file
and folder in this folder.

If it is a file, print
out the name.

If it is a folder, add
it to the queue of
folders to search.

Here, we use a queue like we did in the mango seller example. In the
queue we keep track of what folders we still need to search. Of course,
in that example, we stopped once we found a mango seller, but here we
go through the whole tree.

There's one other important difference from the mango seller code. Can
you spot it?

In the mango seller example, remember we had to keep track of
whether we had already searched a person:

```python
...
    if person not in searched:
        if person_is_seller(person):
...
```

Only search this person
if you haven't already
searched them.

NO CYCLES

NO
MULTIPLE
PARENTS

We don't have to do that here! Trees
don't have cycles, and each node only
has one parent. There's no way we would
accidentally search the same folder more
than once or end up in an infinite loop,
so there's no need to keep track of which
folders we have already searched. There
simply isn't a way to revisit a folder.

This property of trees has made our code simpler. That's an important takeaway from this chapter: trees don't have cycles.

A note on symbolic links

You may know what symbolic links are. If you don't, symbolic links are a way to introduce a cycle in a file directory. I could make a symbolic link on macOS or Linux with

```
ln -s pics/ pics/2001/pics
```

or, on Windows, with

```
mklink /d pics/ pics/2001/pics
```

If I did that, the tree would look like the following.

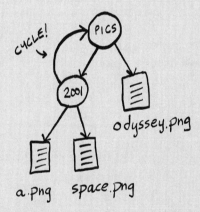

Now our file directory isn't a tree anymore! To keep things simple, for this example, we are going to ignore symbolic links. If we did have a symbolic link, Python is smart enough to avoid an infinite loop. Here is the error it throws:

```
OSError: [Errno 62] Too many levels of symbolic links:
'pics/2001/pics'
```

A space odyssey:
Depth-first search

Let's traverse our file directory again, doing it recursively this time:

```
from os import listdir
from os.path import isfile, join

def printnames(dir):
    for file in sorted(listdir(dir)):        ◄········  Loop through every
        fullpath = join(dir, file)                      file and folder in
        if isfile(fullpath):                            the current folder.
            print(file)      ◄·········  If it is a file, print
        else:                            out the name.
            printnames(fullpath)        ◄·········  If it is a folder, call this
                                                     function recursively on it to
printnames("pics")                                   look for files and folders.
```

Notice that now we are not using a queue. Instead, when we come across a folder, we immediately look inside for more files and folders. Now we have two ways of listing the file names. But here's the surprising part: *the solutions will print the file names in different orders!*

One prints the names out like this:

```
a.png
space.png
odyssey.png
```

The other prints this:

```
odyssey.png
a.png
space.png
```

Can you figure out which solution prints which order and why? Try it yourself before moving on.

The first solution uses breadth-first search. When it finds a folder, that folder is added to the queue to be checked later. So the algorithm goes to the 2001 folder, does not go into it but adds it to the queue to be looked at later, prints all the file names in the pics/ folder, and then goes back to the 2001/ folder and prints the file names in there.

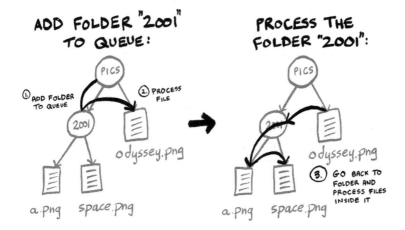

You can see the algorithm visits the 2001 folder first but doesn't look inside. That folder is just added to the queue, and breadth-first search moves on to odyssey.png.

The second solution uses an algorithm called depth-first search. Depth-first search is also a graph and tree traversal algorithm. When it finds a folder, it looks inside immediately instead of adding it to a queue.

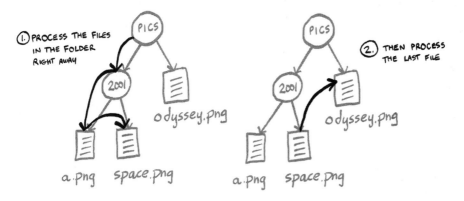

The second solution is the one that prints out

```
a.png
space.png
odyssey.png
```

Breadth-first search and depth-first search are closely related, and often where one is mentioned, the other will be also. Both algorithms printed out all the file names, so they both work for this example. But there is a big difference. Depth-first search cannot be used for finding the shortest path!

In the mango seller example, we could not have used depth-first search. We rely on the fact that we are checking all our first-degree friends before our second-degree friends, and so on. That's what breadth-first search does. But depth-first search will go as deep as possible right away. It may find you a mango seller three degrees away when you have a closer contact! Suppose the following is your social network.

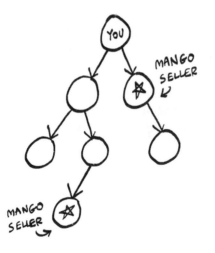

Let's say we process nodes in order from left to right. Depth-first search will get to the leftmost child node and go deep.

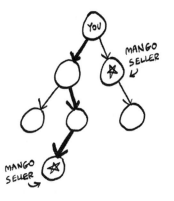

Because the depth-first search went deep on the left node, it failed to realize that the right node is a mango seller that is much closer.

Breadth-first search will correctly find the closest mango seller.

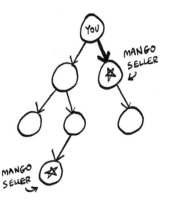

So while both algorithms worked for listing files, only breadth-first search works for finding the shortest path. Depth-first search has other uses. It can be used to find the topological sort, a concept we saw briefly in chapter 6.

A better definition of trees

Now that you have seen an example, it's time for a better definition of a
tree. A tree is a *connected, acyclic graph*.

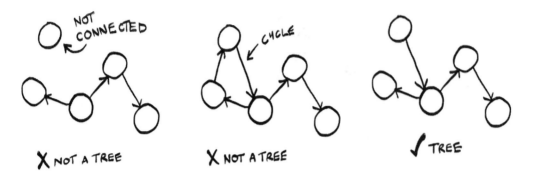

As I had said earlier, we are working exclusively with rooted trees, so
our trees all have a root as well. And we are working exclusively with
connected graphs. So the most important thing to remember is *trees
cannot have cycles.*

Now we have seen a tree in action, let's zoom in on one specific type of
tree.

Binary trees

Computer science is full of different types of trees. Binary trees are a very common type of tree. For the rest of this chapter and most of the next, we will work with binary trees.

A binary tree is a special type of tree where nodes can have at most two children (hence the name *binary*, meaning *two*). These are traditionally called left child and right child.

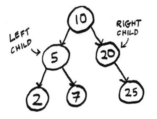

An ancestry tree is an example of a binary tree since everyone has two biological parents.

In that example, there's a clear connection between nodes—they are all family. However, the data can be totally arbitrary.

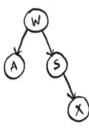

The important thing is you never have more than two children. Sometimes people refer to the left subtree or right subtree.

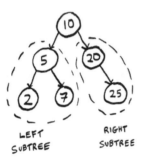

Binary trees show up everywhere in computer science. We are going to spend the rest of this chapter looking at an example that uses a binary tree.

Huffman coding

Huffman coding is a neat example of using binary trees. It's also the foundation for text compression algorithms. We won't describe the algorithm but will spend time focusing on how it works and how it makes clever use of trees.

First, a little background. To know how compression works, we need to know how much space a text file takes. Suppose we have a text file with just one word: *tilt*. How much space does that use? You can use the stat command (available on Unix). First, save the word in a file called test. txt. Then, using stat,

```
$ cat test.txt
tilt

$ stat -f%z test.txt
4
```

so that file takes up 4 bytes: 1 byte per character.

This makes sense. Assuming we are using ISO-8859-1 (see the following sidebar for what this means), each letter takes up exactly 1 byte. For example, the letter *a* is ISO-8859-1 code 97, which I can write in binary as 01100001. That is 8 bits. A bit is a digit that can be either 0 or 1. And there are eight of them. Eight bits is 1 byte. So the letter *a* is represented using 1 byte. ISO-8859-1 code goes from 00000000, which represents the null character, all the way to 11111111, which represents ÿ (Latin lowercase letter *y* with diaeresis). There are 256 possible combinations of 0s and 1s with 8 bits, so the ISO-8859-1 code allows for 256 possible letters.

Character encoding

As this example will show you, there are many different ways to encode characters. That is, the letter *a* could be written in binary in many different ways.

It started with ASCII. In the 1960s, ASCII was created. ASCII is a 7-bit encoding. Unfortunately, ASCII did not include a lot of characters. ASCII does not include any characters with umlauts (*ü* or *ö*, for example) or common currencies like the British pound or Japanese yen.

So ISO-8859-1 was created. ISO-8859-1 is an 8-bit encoding, so it doubles the number of characters that ASCII provided. We went from 128 characters to 256 characters. But this was still not enough, and countries began making their own encodings. For example, Japan has several encodings for Japanese since ISO-8859-1 and ASCII were focused on European languages. The whole situation was a mess until Unicode was introduced.

Unicode is an encoding standard. It aims to provide characters for any language. Unicode has 149,186 characters as of version 15—quite a jump from 256! More than 1,000 of these are emojis.

Unicode is the standard, but you need to use an encoding that follows the standard. The most popular encoding today is UTF-8. UTF-8 is variable-length character encoding, which means characters can be anywhere from 1 to 4 bytes (8–32 bits).

You don't need to worry too much about this. I've kept the example simple intentionally by using ISO-8859-1, which is 8 bits—a nice consistent quantity of bits to work with.

Just remember these takeaways:

- Compression algorithms try to reduce the number of bits needed to store each character.

- If you need to pick an encoding for a project, UTF-8 is a good default choice.

Let's decode some binary to ISO-8859-1 together: 011100100110000101100100. You can Google an ISO-8859-1 table or a binary-to-ISO-8859-1 converter to make this easier.

First, we know that each letter is 8 bits, so I am going to divide this into chunks of 8 bits to make it easier to read:

```
01110010 01100001 01100100
```

Great, now we see that there are three letters. Looking them up in an ISO-8859-1 table, I see they spell out rad: 01110010 is r, and so on. This is how your text editor takes the binary data in a text file and displays it as ISO-8859-1. You can view the binary information by using xxd. This utility is available on Unix. Here is how tilt looks in binary:

```
$ xxd -b test.txt
00000000: 01110100  01101001  01101100  01110100
tilt
```

Here is where the compression comes in. For the word *tilt*, we don't need 256 possible letters; we just need three. So we don't need 8 bits; we only need 2. We could come up with our own 2-bit code just for these three letters:

```
t = 00
i = 01
l = 10
```

Here is how we could write *tilt* using our new code: 00011000. I can make this easier to read by adding spaces again: 00 01 10 00. If you compare it to the mapping, you'll see this spells out *tilt*.

This is what Huffman coding does: it looks at the characters being used and tries to use less than 8 bits. That is how it compresses the data. Huffman coding generates a tree.

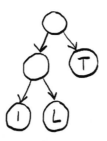

You can use this tree to find the code for each letter. Starting at the root node, find a path down to the letter *L*. Whenever you choose a left branch, append a 0 to your code. When you choose a right branch, append 1. When you get to a letter, stop progressing down the tree. So the code for the letter *L* is 01. Here are the three codes given by the tree:

```
i = 00
l = 01
t = 1
```

Notice that the letter T has a code of just one digit. Unlike ISO-8859-1, *in Huffman coding, the codes don't all have to be the same length.* This is important. Let's see another example to understand why.

Now we want to compress the phrase "paranoid android." Here is the tree generated by the Huffman coding algorithm.

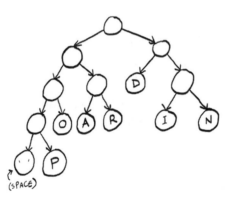

Check yourself: What is the code for the letter *P*? Try it yourself before reading on. It is 0001. What about the letter *D*? It is 10.

In this case, there are actually three different possible lengths! Suppose

we try to decode some binary data: 01101010. We see the problem right away: we can't chunk this up the way we did with ISO-8859-1! While all ISO-8859-1 codes were eight digits, here the code could be two, three, or four digits. *Since the code length varies, we can't use chunking anymore.*

Instead, we need to look at one digit at a time, as if we are looking at a tape.

Here's how to do it: first number is 0, so go left (I'm only showing part of the tree here).

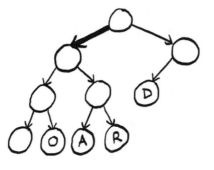

Then we get a 1, so we go right.

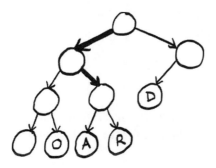

Then we get another 1, so we go right again.

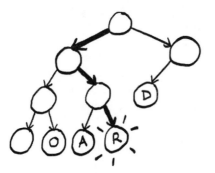

Aha! We found a letter. This is the binary data we have left: 01010. We can start over at the root node and find the other letters. Try decoding the rest yourself and then read on. Did you get the word? It was *rad*. This is a big difference between Huffman coding and ISO-8859-1. The codes can vary, so the decoding needs to be done differently.

It is more work to do it this way instead of chunking. But there is one big benefit. Notice that the letters that show up more often have shorter codes. *D* appears three times, so its code is just two digits versus *I*, which appears twice, and *P*, which appears only once. Instead of assigning 4 bits to everything, we can compress frequently used letters even more. You can see how, in a longer piece of text, this would be a big savings!

Now that we understand at a high level how Huffman coding works, let's see what properties of trees Huffman is taking advantage of here.

First, could there be overlap between codes? Take this code for example:

```
a = 0
b = 1
c = 00
```

Now if you see the binary 001, is that *AAB* or *CB*? *c* and *a* share part of their code, so it's unclear. Here is what the tree for this code would look like.

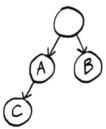

We pass A on the way to C, which causes the problem.

That's not a problem with Huffman coding because letters only show up at leaf nodes. And there's a unique path from the root to each leaf node—that's one of the properties of trees. So we can guarantee overlap is not a problem.

This also guarantees there is only one code for each letter. Having multiple paths to each letter would mean there are multiple codes assigned to each letter, which would be unnecessary.

When we read the code one digit at a time, we are assuming we will eventually end up at a letter. If this was a graph with a cycle, we couldn't make that assumption. We could get stuck in the cycle and end up in an infinite loop.

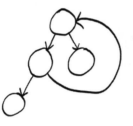

But since this is a tree, we know there are no cycles, so we are guaranteed to end up at some letter.

We are using a rooted tree. Rooted trees have a root node, which is important because we need to know where to start! Graphs do not necessarily have a root node.

Finally, the type of tree used here is called a *binary tree*. Binary trees can have at most two children—the left child and the right child. This makes sense because binary only has two digits. If there was a third child, it would be unclear what digit it is supposed to represent.

This chapter introduced you to trees. In the next chapter, we will see some different types of trees and what they are used for.

Recap

- Trees are a type of graph, but trees don't have cycles.

- Depth-first search is another graph traversal algorithm. It can't be used to find shortest paths.

- A binary tree is a special type of tree where nodes can have, at most, two children.

- There are many different types of character encodings. Unicode is the international standard, and UTF-8 is the most common Unicode encoding.

In this chapter

- You learn about a new data structure called binary search trees (BSTs).

- You learn about balanced trees and why they often perform better than arrays or linked lists.

- You also learn about AVL trees, a type of balanced BST. In the worst-case scenario, binary trees can be slow. A balanced tree will help them perform effectively.

In the last chapter, you learned about the new data structure, trees. Now that you and trees are best friends, it's time to see what they are used for. When arrays and linked lists fail to deliver the desired performance, a good next step is to try a tree. In this chapter, we'll discuss the performance that trees can offer. We'll then explore a special type of tree that can offer exceptional performance, called a balanced tree.

A balancing act

Remember binary search from way back in chapter 1? Using binary search, we are able to find information much more quickly than if we did a simple search using O(log n) instead of O(n). There is one problem, though: insertion. Sure, searching takes O(log n) time, but the array needs to be sorted. If you want to insert a new number into your sorted array, it will take O(n) time. The issue is making a spot for the new value. You need to move a bunch of values to make room.

If only we could insert like we do in a linked list, where we just need to change a couple of pointers.

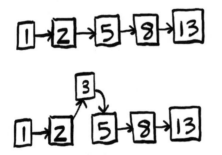

But searching is linear time in linked lists. How can we get the best of both worlds?

Improving insertion speed with trees

So we really want the search speed of a sorted array with a faster insertion speed. We know that insertions are faster in linked lists. So we want some kind of data structure that combines these ideas.

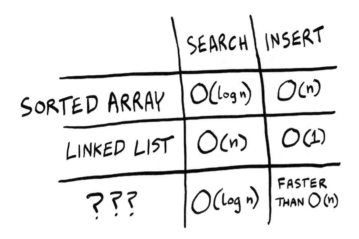

	SEARCH	INSERT
SORTED ARRAY	$O(\log n)$	$O(n)$
LINKED LIST	$O(n)$	$O(1)$
???	$O(\log n)$	FASTER THAN $O(n)$

And that structure is a tree! There are dozens of different types of trees to choose from, so I specifically mean a balanced binary search tree (BST). In this chapter, we will see how a BST works, and then we will learn how to balance it.

BSTs are a type of binary tree. Here is an example of a BST.

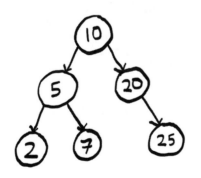

Just like a binary tree, each node has up to two children: the left child and the right child. But it has a special property that makes it a BST: the value of the left child is *always smaller* than the node, and the value of the right child is *always greater*. So for node 10, its left child has a smaller value (5), and its right child has a bigger value (20).

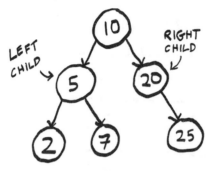

Not only that, all the numbers in the left child subtree are smaller than the node!

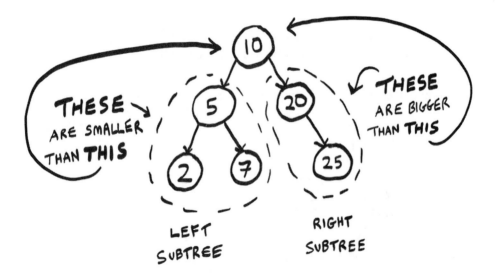

This special property means searches will be very fast.

Let's see if the number 7 is in this tree. Here is how we do it. Start at the root node.

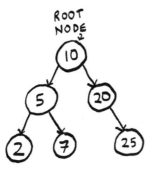

Seven is smaller than 10, so we check the left subtree. Remember, all the nodes with smaller values are on the left, and all the nodes with bigger values are on the right. So we know right away we don't need to check the nodes on the right since 7 won't be there. If we go left from the 10, we get to the 5.

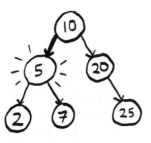

Seven is bigger than 5, so let's go right this time.

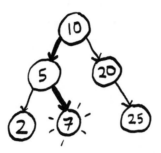

We found it! Now let's look for another number, 8. We follow the exact same path.

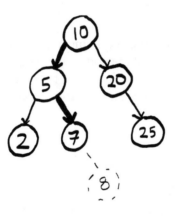

Except now it is not there! If it was in the tree, it would be right where the dotted node is. The whole reason we are talking about trees is to see if they are faster than arrays and linked lists. So let's talk about the performance of this tree. To do that, we need to look at the height of the tree.

Shorter trees are faster

Let's look at two trees. They both have seven nodes, but the performance is very different.

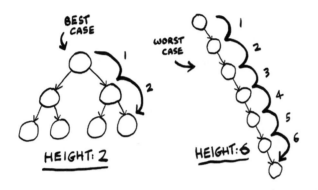

The height of the best-case tree is 2. This means you can get to any node from the root node in, at most, two steps. The height of the worst-case tree is 6. This means you can get to any node from the root node in, at most, *six* steps. Let's compare this to the performance of binary search versus simple search. Just to remind you, here's the performance of binary search versus simple search:

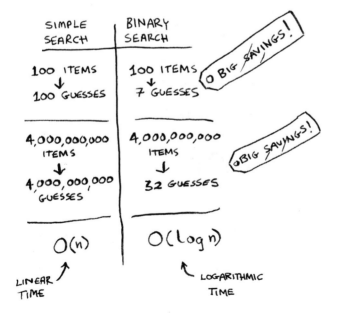

Remember our number guessing game? To guess a number out of 100 numbers, it would take 7 guesses with binary search, but 100 guesses with simple search. Well, we're in a similar situation with trees.

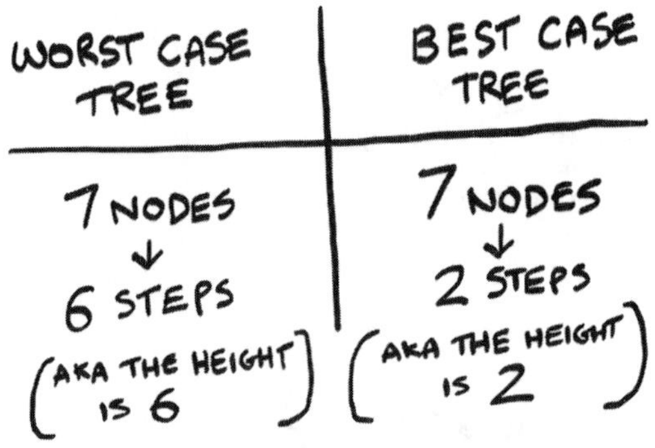

WORST CASE TREE | BEST CASE TREE

7 NODES
↓
6 STEPS
(AKA THE HEIGHT IS 6)

7 NODES
↓
2 STEPS
(AKA THE HEIGHT IS 2)

The worst-case tree is taller, and it has worse performance. In the worst-case tree, the nodes are all in a line. This tree has height $O(n)$, so searches will take $O(n)$ time. You can think of it this way: this tree is really just a linked list since one node points to another, and so on, in a line. And searching through a linked list takes $O(n)$ time.

The best-case tree has height $O(\log n)$, and searching this tree will take $O(\log n)$ time.

WORST CASE TREE | BEST CASE TREE

7 NODES
↓
6 STEPS

7 NODES
↓
2 STEPS

SEARCH TIME: $O(n)$ | $O(\log n)$

So this situation is very similar to binary search versus simple search! *If we can guarantee the height of our tree will be O(log n)*, then searching the tree will be O(log *n*), just like we wanted.

	SEARCH	INSERT
SORTED ARRAY	$O(\log n)$	$O(n)$
LINKED LIST	$O(n)$	$O(1)$
???	$O(\log n)$	FASTER THAN $O(n)$

But how can we guarantee the height will be O(log *n*)? Here's an example where we build a tree that ends up being a worst-case tree (something we want to avoid). We will start with one node.

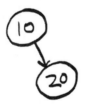

Let's add another one.

So far, so good. Let's add a few more.

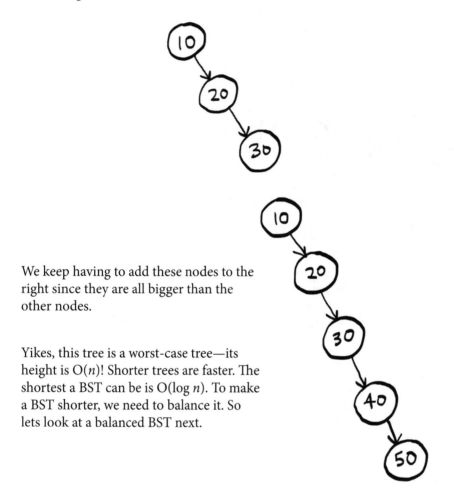

We keep having to add these nodes to the right since they are all bigger than the other nodes.

Yikes, this tree is a worst-case tree—its height is O(n)! Shorter trees are faster. The shortest a BST can be is O(log n). To make a BST shorter, we need to balance it. So lets look at a balanced BST next.

AVL trees: A type of balanced tree

AVL trees are a type of self-balancing BST. This means AVL trees will maintain a height of O(log *n*). Whenever the tree is out of balance—that is, the height is not O(log *n*)—it will correct itself. For the last example, the tree may balance itself to look like this.

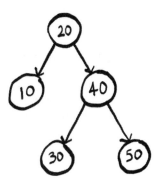

An AVL tree will give us that O(log *n*) height we want by balancing itself through rotations.

Rotations

Suppose you have a tree with three nodes. Any one of them could be the root node.

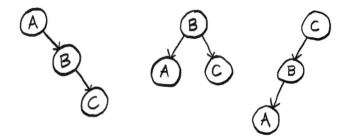

You use rotation to move a set of nodes to end up with a new arrangement. Let's see a rotation in slow motion.

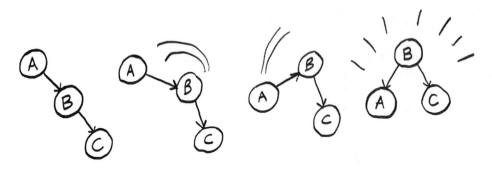

We rotated to the left. We started with an unbalanced tree with A as the root node and ended up with a balanced tree with B as the root node.

Rotations are a popular way to balance trees. AVL trees use rotation to balance. Let's see an example. We'll start with one node again.

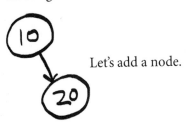   Let's add a node.

So far, so good. The children aren't exactly the same height; there's a difference of 1. But a difference of 1 is OK for AVL trees. Now we will add one more.

Uh oh! Now the tree is unbalanced. Time to rotate!

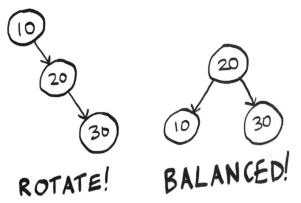

We did a left rotation, and now the tree is balanced again.

Let's add one more node.

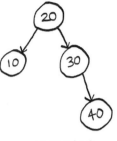

And add another node.

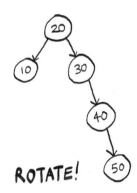

We need to rotate again!

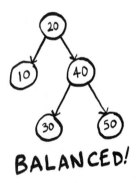

Phew. Using rotation, the AVL tree has balanced itself. Notice in that last example, the node "30" got rotated instead of the node "20". There's an example coming up that explains why.

How does the AVL tree know when it's time to rotate?

We can see visually that the tree is off balance—one side is longer than the other. But how does the tree know that?

For the tree to know when it's time to balance itself, it needs to store some extra information. Each node stores one of two pieces of information: its height or something called a *balance factor*. The balance factor can be −1, 0, or 1.

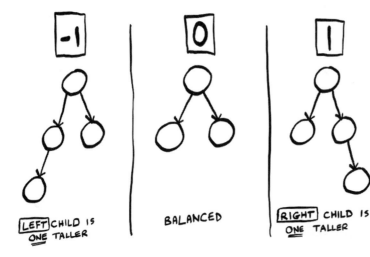

Note that this image shows you the balance factors for the root nodes only, but you would need to store the balance factor for each node (I'll show an example of this shortly).

The balance factor tells you which child is taller and by how much. The balance factor lets the tree know when to rebalance. Zero means the tree is balanced. A −1 or 1 is OK, too, because remember, AVL trees don't have to be perfectly balanced: a difference of one is OK.

But if the balance factor drops below −1 or moves above 1, it's time to rebalance. To the right are two trees that need rebalancing.

LEFT CHILD IS
TWO TALLER !!

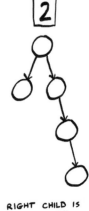

RIGHT CHILD IS
TWO TALLER!!

As I said, each node needs to store either the height or the balance factor. In my example, I am going to store both so you can see how they both change. But if you have the heights of each subtree, it is easy to compute the balance factor. Let's see an example. Take this tree.

We are going to add this node to it.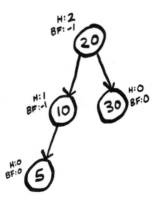

First, let's write out the height and balance factors for each node. In this image, H is height, and BF is balance factor.

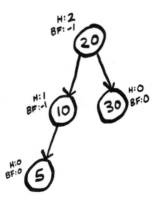

Remember, I am storing both values to show how they change, but you would only need to store one. Make sure these numbers make sense to you. Note that all the leaf nodes have a balance factor of 0: they have no child nodes, so there's nothing to keep in balance.

Now let's add the new node.

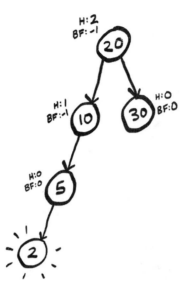

After adding this node, we need to set its height and balance factor.
Then we can go up the tree, updating the heights and balance factors for
all its ancestors.

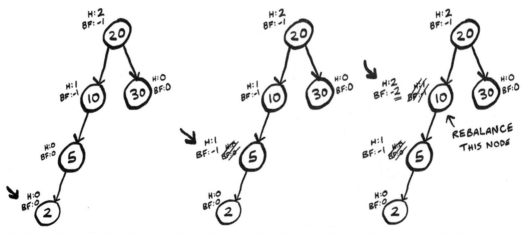

Set the height and balance factor.   Go up the tree and update the height and balance factor for the ancestors.

Aha! We just set the balance factor to −2, which means it's time to rotate! I will show the rest of the example next, but this is the main takeaway: after an insert, you update the balance factors for that node's ancestors. The AVL tree looks at the balance factor to know when it needs to rebalance. Finishing the example, let's rotate the 10.

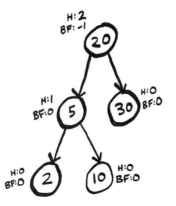

Now that subtree is balanced. Let's keep moving up the tree.

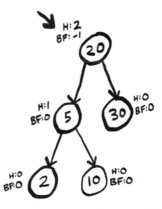

Nothing to update there. We actually didn't need to keep moving up the tree because AVL trees require, at most, one rebalancing.

AVL trees are a good option if you want a balanced BST. Let's recap our journey:

- Binary trees are a type of tree.

- In binary trees, each node has, at most, two children.

- BSTs are a type of binary tree where all the values in the left subtree are smaller than the node, and all the values in the right are greater than the node.

- BSTs can give great performance if we can guarantee their height will be O(log *n*).

- AVL trees are self-balancing BSTs, guaranteeing their height will be O(log *n*).

- AVL trees balance themselves through rotations.

We haven't covered everything. We have covered one case for rotations, and there are other cases. We won't spend time digging into them, as you will rarely need to implement an AVL tree yourself.

Now we know AVL trees offer O(log *n*) search performance. What about insertions? Well, insertions are just a matter of searching for a place to insert the node and adding a pointer, just like a linked list. For example, if we want to insert an 8 in this tree, we just need to find where to add the pointer.

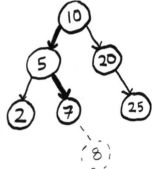

So insertions are O(log *n*) as well.

At the start of this chapter, we were looking for a data structure that offered both fast searches and fast inserts. We have found our magic data structure: it's a balanced BST!

	SEARCH	INSERT
SORTED ARRAY	O(log n)	O(n)
LINKED LIST	O(n)	O(1)
BST	O(log n)	O(log n)

Splay trees

AVL trees are a good basic balanced BST that guarantees O(log *n*) time for a bunch of operations.

Splay trees are a different take on balanced BSTs. The cool thing about splay trees is if you have recently looked up an item, the next time you look it up, the lookup will be faster. There is something intuitively pleasing about this. For example, suppose you have some software where you give it a zip code, and it will look up the city for you.

You can picture the interaction going like this.

Now suppose you are repeatedly looking up the same zip code.

That feels sort of silly.

The software just looked up the zip code; why can't it remember that? It should really go something like this.

This is what splay trees allow you to do. When you look up a node in a splay tree, it will make that node the new root, so if you look it up again, the lookup will be instant. In general, the nodes you have looked up recently get clustered to the top and become faster to look up.

The tradeoff is the tree is not guaranteed to be balanced. So *some* searches might take longer than O(log *n*) time. Some searches may take as long as linear time! Also, while performing the search, you may have to rotate the node up to the root if it is not already the root, and that will take time.

But we are OK with the tradeoff of not having a balanced tree all the time. Because the cool thing is that if you do n searches, the total time is O(*n* log *n*) *guaranteed*—that is, O(log *n*) per search. So even though a single search may take longer than O(log *n*) time, overall, they will average out to O(log *n*) time, and the faster search time is our goal.

B-trees

B-trees are a generalized form of binary tree. They are often used for building databases. Here is a B-tree.

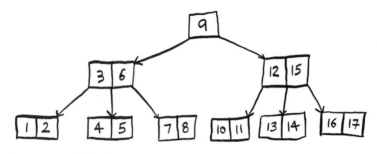

Looks pretty wild, huh? You may notice that some of these nodes have more than two children.

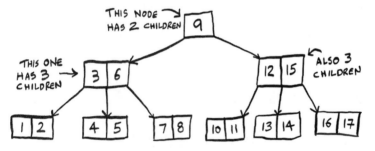

Unlike binary trees, B-trees can have many more children.

You've probably also noticed that, unlike our previous trees, most nodes have two keys.

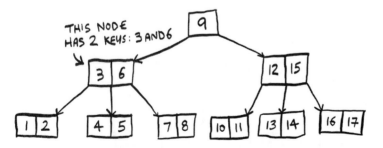

So not only can nodes in B-trees have more than two children, they can have more than one key! This is why I said B-trees are a generalized form of BSTs.

What is the advantage of B-trees?

B-trees have a very interesting optimization because it's a physical optimization. Computers are physical objects. So when we are looking things up in a tree, a physical object has to move to retrieve that data. This is called *seek time*. Seek time can be a big factor in how fast or slow your algorithm is.

Think of it like going to the grocery store. You could go shopping for one item at a time. Suppose you decide to buy milk. After coming home, you realize you should get some bread, too, so you go back to the store. After coming home again, you realize you're out of coffee. So you go back to the store again. What an inefficient way to shop! It would be much better to shop once and buy a bunch of stuff while you are there. In this example, driving to and from the store is the seek time.

The fundamental idea with B-Trees is that *once you've done the seek, you might as well read a bunch of stuff into memory*. That is, once you're at the store, you might as well buy everything you need instead of going back repeatedly.

B-trees have bigger nodes: each node can have many more keys and children than a binary tree. So we spend more time reading each node. *But we seek less because we read more data in one go.* This is what makes B-trees faster.

B-trees are a popular data structure for databases, which is no surprise as databases spend a lot of time retrieving data from disk.

Notice the ordering in a B-tree; it is pretty interesting, too. You start at the lower left.

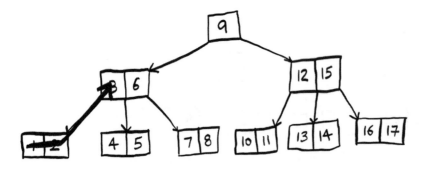

Where do you go from here?

You'll snake across the whole tree.

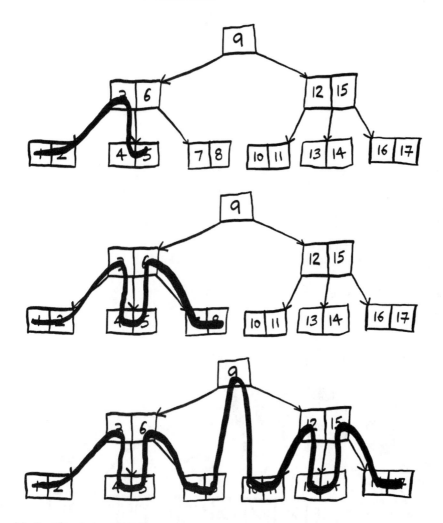

Notice that it is still following the property of the BST, where for each key, the keys to the left are smaller, and the keys to the right are bigger. For example, for key 3, the keys to the left are 1 and 2, and the keys to the right are 4 and 5.

Also notice that the number of children is one greater than the number of keys. So the root node has one key and two children. Each of those children has two keys and three children.

That concludes our two chapters on trees. It's unlikely you will need to implement a tree yourself, but it's important to know that trees are a type of graph, and they offer great performance. In the next chapter, we will return to graphs and talk about a new type of graph: a weighted graph.

Recap

- Balanced binary search trees (BSTs) offer the same Big O search performance as arrays with better insertion performance.

- The height of a tree affects its performance.

- AVL trees are a popular type of balanced BST. Like most balanced trees, AVL trees balance themselves through rotation.

- B-trees are generalized BSTs, where each node can have multiple keys and multiple child nodes.

- Seek time is like travel time to a grocery store. B-trees try to minimize seek time by reading more data in one go.

In this chapter

- We continue the discussion of graphs, and you learn about weighted graphs, a way to assign more or less weight to some edges.

- You learn Dijkstra's algorithm, which lets you answer "What's the shortest path to X?" for weighted graphs.

- You learn about negative-weight edges in graphs, where Dijkstra's algorithm doesn't work.

In chapter 6, you figured out a way to get from point A to point B.

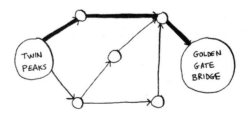

It's not necessarily the fastest path. It's the shortest path because it has the least number of segments (three segments). But suppose you add travel times to those segments. Now you see that there's a faster path.

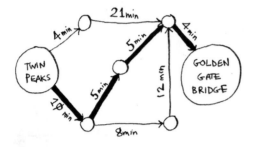

You used breadth-first search in chapter 6. Breadth-first search will find the path with the fewest segments (the first graph shown here). What if you want the fastest path instead (the second graph)? You can do that *fastest* with a different algorithm called *Dijkstra's algorithm*.

Working with Dijkstra's algorithm

Let's see how it works with this graph.

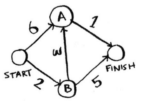

Each segment has a travel time in minutes. You'll use Dijkstra's algorithm to go from Start to Finish in the shortest possible time.

If you ran breadth-first search on this graph, you'd get this shortest path.

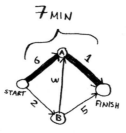

But that path takes 7 minutes. Let's see if you can find a path that takes less time! There are four steps to Dijkstra's algorithm:

1. Find the "cheapest" node. This is the node you can get to in the least amount of time.

2. Update the costs of the out-neighbors of this node. I'll explain what I mean by this shortly.

3. Repeat until you've done this for every node in the graph.

4. Calculate the final path.

Step 1: Find the cheapest node. You're standing at Start, wondering if you should go to node A or node B. How long does it take to get to each node?

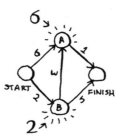

It takes 6 minutes to get to node A and 2 minutes to get to node B. The rest of the nodes, you don't know yet.

Because you don't know how long it takes to get to Finish yet, you put down infinity (you'll see why soon). Node B is the closest node—it's 2 minutes away.

NODE	TIME TO NODE
A	6
B	2
FINISH	∞

Step 2: Calculate how long it takes to get to all of node B's out-neighbors *by following an edge from B.*

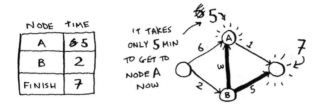

Hey, you just found a shorter path to node A! It used to take 6 minutes to get to node A.

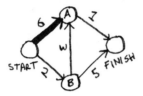

But if you go through node B, there's a path that only takes 5 minutes!

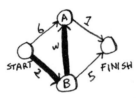

When you find a shorter path for a neighbor of B, update its cost. In this case, you found

- A shorter path to A (down from 6 minutes to 5 minutes)

- A shorter path to Finish (down from infinity to 7 minutes)

Step 3: Repeat.

Step 1 again: Find the node that takes the least amount of time to get to. You're done with node B, so node A has the next smallest time estimate.

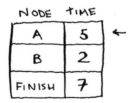

Step 2 again: Update the costs for node A's out-neighbors.

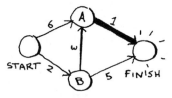

Woo, it takes 6 minutes to get to Finish now!

You've run Dijkstra's algorithm for every node (you don't need to run it for the Finish node). At this point, you know

- It takes 2 minutes to get to node B.
- It takes 5 minutes to get to node A.
- It takes 6 minutes to get to Finish.

NODE	TIME
A	5
B	2
FINISH	6

I'll save the last step, calculating the final path, for the next section. For now, I'll just show you what the final path is.

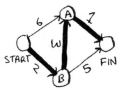

Breadth-first search wouldn't have found this as the shortest path because it has three segments. And there's a way to get from Start to Finish in two segments.

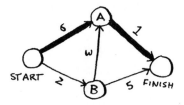

SHORTEST PATH
WITH BREADTH-FIRST SEARCH

In the last chapter, you used breadth-first search to find the shortest path between two points. Back then, "shortest path" meant the path with the fewest segments. But in Dijkstra's algorithm, you assign a number or weight to each segment. Then Dijkstra's algorithm finds the path with the smallest total weight.

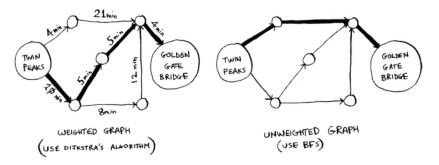

To recap, Dijkstra's algorithm has four steps:

1.   Find the cheapest node. This is the node you can get to in the least amount of time.

2.   Check whether there's a cheaper path to the out-neighbors of this node. If so, update their costs.

3.   Repeat until you've done this for every node in the graph.

4.   Calculate the final path. (Coming up in the next section!)

Terminology

I want to show you some more examples of Dijkstra's algorithm in action. But, first, let me clarify some terminology.

When you work with Dijkstra's algorithm, each edge in the graph has a number associated with it. These are called *weights*.

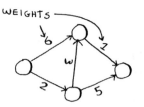

A graph with weights is called a *weighted graph*. A graph without weights is called an *unweighted graph*.

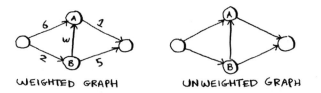

WEIGHTED GRAPH   UNWEIGHTED GRAPH

To calculate the shortest path in an unweighted graph, use *breadth-first search*. To calculate the shortest path in a weighted graph, use *Dijkstra's algorithm*. Graphs can also have *cycles*. A cycle looks like this.

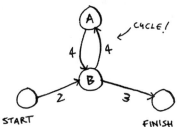

It means you can start at a node, travel around, and end up at the same node. Suppose you're trying to find the shortest path in this graph that has a cycle.

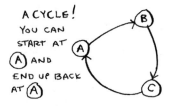

Would it make sense to follow the cycle? Well, you can use the path that avoids the cycle.

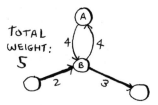

Or you can follow the cycle.

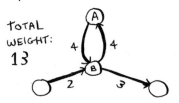

You end up at the target node either way, but the cycle adds more
weight. You could even follow the cycle twice if you wanted.

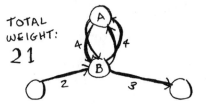

But every time you follow the cycle, you're just adding 8 to the total
weight. So following the cycle will never give you the shortest path.

Finally, remember our conversation about directed versus undirected
graphs from chapter 6?

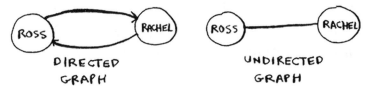

An undirected graph means that both nodes point to each other. That's
a cycle!

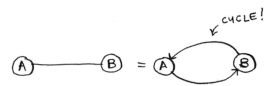

With an undirected graph, each edge adds another cycle. Dijkstra's
algorithm only works on graphs with no cycles, where all the edges
are nonnegative. Yes, it's possible for graph edges to have a negative
weight! But Dijkstra's algorithm won't work—in that case, you'll need
an algorithm called Bellman–Ford. There's a section on negative weight
edges coming later in the chapter.

Trading for a piano

Enough terminology, let's look at another example! This
is Rama.

Rama is trying to trade a music book for a piano.

"I'll give you this poster for your book," says Alex. "It's a poster of my favorite band, Destroyer. Or I'll give you this rare LP of Rick Astley for your book and $5 more." "Ooh, I've heard that LP has a really great song," says Amy. "I'll trade you my guitar or drum set for the poster or the LP."

"I've been meaning to get into guitar!" exclaims Beethoven. "Hey, I'll trade you my piano for either of Amy's things."

Perfect! With a little bit of money, Rama can trade his way from a piano book to a real piano. Now he just needs to figure out how to spend the least amount of money to make those trades. Let's graph out what he's been offered.

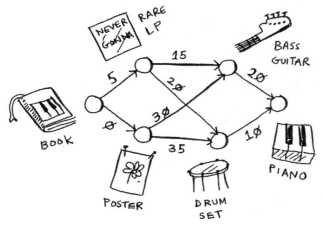

In this graph, the nodes are all the items Rama can trade for. The weights on the edges are the amount of money he would have to pay to make the trade. So he can trade the poster for the guitar for $30 or trade the LP for the guitar for $15. How is Rama going to figure out the path from the book to the piano where he spends the least dough? Dijkstra's algorithm to the rescue! Remember, Dijkstra's algorithm has four steps. In this example, you'll do all four steps, so you'll calculate the final path at the end, too.

NODE	COST
LP	5
POSTER	0
GUITAR	∞
DRUMS	∞
PIANO	∞

} WE HAVEN'T REACHED THESE NODES FROM THE START YET

Before you start, you need some setup. Make a table of the cost for each node. The cost of a node is how expensive it is to get to.

You'll keep updating this table as the algorithm goes on. To calculate the final path, you also need a *parent* column on this table.

NODE	PARENT
LP	BOOK
POSTER	BOOK
GUITAR	—
DRUMS	—
PIANO	—

I'll show you how this column works soon. Let's start the algorithm.

Step 1: Find the cheapest node. In this case, the poster is the cheapest trade at $0. Is there a cheaper way to trade for the poster? This is a really important point, so think about it. Can you see a series of trades that will get Rama the poster for less than $0? Read on when you're ready. Answer: No. *Because the poster is the cheapest node Rama can get to, there's no way to make it any cheaper.* Here's a different way to look at it. Suppose you're traveling from home to work.

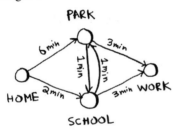

If you take the path toward the school, that takes 2 minutes. If you take the path toward the park, that takes 6 minutes. Is there any way you can take the path toward the park and end up at the school in less than 2 minutes? It's impossible because it takes longer than 2 minutes just to get to the park. On the other hand, can you find a faster path to the park? Yup.

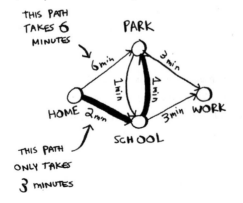

This is the key idea behind Dijkstra's algorithm: look at the cheapest node on your graph. There is no cheaper way to get to this node!

Back to the music example. The poster is the cheapest trade.

Step 2: Figure out how long it takes to get to its out-neighbors (the cost).

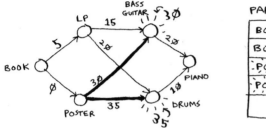

PARENT	NODE	COST
BOOK	LP	5
BOOK	POSTER	∅
POSTER	GUITAR	~~$~~ ~~30~~
POSTER	DRUMS	~~∅∅~~ ~~35~~
—	PIANO	∞

You have prices for the bass guitar and the drum set in the table. Their value was set when you went through the poster, so the poster gets set as their parent. That means, to get to the bass guitar, you follow the edge from the poster, and the same for the drums.

	PARENT	NODE	COST
	BOOK	LP	5
	BOOK	POSTER	∅
WE GO FROM "POSTER" TO GET TO THESE NODES	POSTER	GUITAR	3∅
	POSTER	DRUMS	35
	—	PIANO	∞

Step 1 again: The LP is the next cheapest node at $5.

Step 2 again: Update the values of all of its out-neighbors.

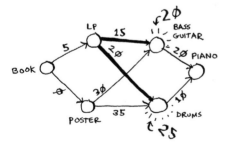

PARENT	NODE	COST
BOOK	LP	5
BOOK	POSTER	∅
LP	GUITAR	~~3∅~~ ~~2∅~~
LP	DRUMS	~~35~~ ~~25~~
—	PIANO	∞

Hey, you updated the price of both the drums and the guitar! That means it's cheaper to get to the drums and guitar by following the edge from the LP. So you set the LP as the new parent for both instruments.

The bass guitar is the next cheapest item. Update its out-neighbors.

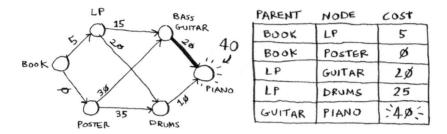

PARENT	NODE	COST
BOOK	LP	5
BOOK	POSTER	∅
LP	GUITAR	2∅
LP	DRUMS	25
GUITAR	PIANO	⁻4∅⁻

OK, you finally have a price for the piano by trading the guitar for the piano. So you set the guitar as the parent. Finally, the last node, the drum set.

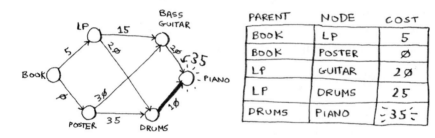

PARENT	NODE	COST
BOOK	LP	5
BOOK	POSTER	∅
LP	GUITAR	2∅
LP	DRUMS	25
DRUMS	PIANO	⁻35⁻

Rama can get the piano even cheaper by trading the drum set for the piano instead. *So the cheapest set of trades will cost Rama $35.*

Now, as I promised, you need to figure out the path. So far, you know that the shortest path costs $35, but how do you figure out the path? To start with, look at the parent for *piano.*

PARENT	NODE
BOOK	LP
BOOK	POSTER
LP	GUITAR
LP	DRUMS
→ DRUMS	PIANO

The piano has drums as its parent. That means Rama trades the drums for the piano. So you follow this edge.

Let's see how you'd follow the edges. *Piano* has *drums* as its parent.

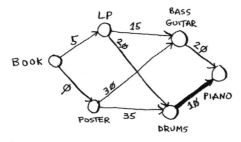

And *drums* has the LP as its parent.

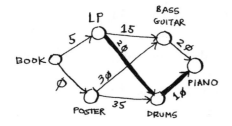

So Rama will trade the LP for the drums. And, of course, he'll trade the book for the LP. By following the parents backward, you now have the complete path.

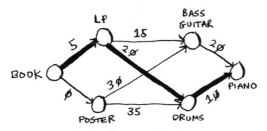

Here's the series of trades Rama needs to make.

So far, I've been using the term *shortest path* pretty literally: calculating the shortest path between two locations or between two people.
I hope this example showed you that the shortest path doesn't have to be about physical distance. It can be about minimizing something. In this case, Rama wanted to minimize the amount of money he spent.
Thanks, Dijkstra!

Negative-weight edges

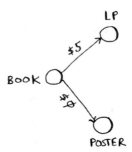

In the trading example, Alex offered to trade the book for two items.

Suppose Sarah offers to trade the LP for the poster, and *she'll give Rama an additional $7*. It doesn't cost Rama anything to make this trade; instead, he gets $7 back.

How would you show this on the graph?

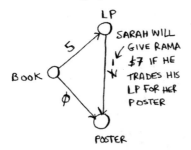

The edge from the LP to the poster has a negative weight! Rama gets $7 back if he makes that trade. Now Rama has two ways to get to the poster.

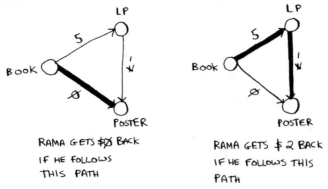

So it makes sense to do the second trade—Rama gets $2 back that way!
Now, if you remember, Rama can trade the poster for the drums. There
are two paths he could take.

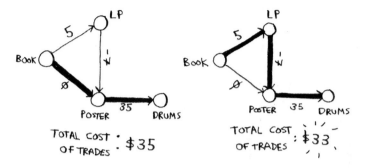

The second path costs him $2 less, so he should take that path, right?
Well, guess what? If you run Dijkstra's algorithm on this graph, Rama
will take the wrong path. He'll take the longer path. *You can't use
Dijkstra's algorithm if you have negative-weight edges.* Negative-weight
edges break the algorithm. Let's see what happens when you run
Dijkstra's algorithm on this. First, make the table of costs.

LP	5
POSTER	∅
DRUMS	∞

COSTS

Next, find the lowest-cost node and update the costs for its out-
neighbors. In this case, the poster is the lowest-cost node. So, according
to Dijkstra's algorithm, *there is no cheaper way to get to the poster than
paying $0* (you know that's wrong!). Anyway, let's update the costs for
its out-neighbors.

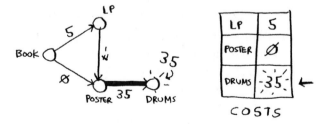

LP	5
POSTER	∅
DRUMS	35

COSTS

OK, the drums have a cost of $35 now.

Let's get the next-cheapest node that hasn't already been processed.

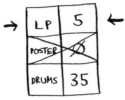

Update the costs for its out-neighbors.

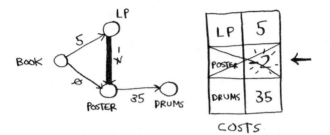

COSTS

You already processed the poster node, but you're updating the cost for it. This is a big red flag. Once you process a node, it means there's no cheaper way to get to that node. But you just found a cheaper way to the poster! Drums doesn't have any out-neighbors, so that's the end of the algorithm. Here are the final costs.

FINAL
COSTS

It costs $35 to get to the drums. You know that there's a path that costs only $33, but Dijkstra's algorithm didn't find it. Dijkstra's algorithm assumed that because you were processing the poster node, there was no cheaper way to get to that node. That assumption only works if you have no negative-weight edges. So you *can't use negative-weight edges with Dijkstra's algorithm.* If you want to find the shortest path in a graph that has negative-weight edges, there's an algorithm for that! It's called the *Bellman–Ford algorithm.* Bellman–Ford is out of the scope of this book, but you can find some great explanations online.

Implementation

Let's see how to implement Dijkstra's algorithm in code. Here's the graph I'll use for the example.

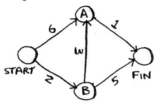

To code this example, you'll need three hash tables.

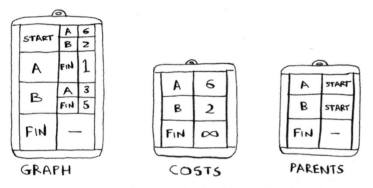

You'll update the costs and parents hash tables as the algorithm progresses. First, you need to implement the graph. You'll use a hash table like you did in chapter 6:

```
graph = {}
```

In the last chapter, you stored all the out-neighbors of a node in the hash table, like this:

```
graph["you"] = ["alice", "bob", "claire"]
```

But this time, you need to store the out-neighbors *and* the cost for getting to that neighbor. For example, Start has two out-neighbors, A and B.

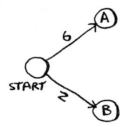

How do you represent the weights of those edges? Why not just use another hash table?

```
graph["start"] = {}
graph["start"]["a"] = 6
graph["start"]["b"] = 2
```

THIS HASH TABLE
HAS MORE HASH TABLES
INSIDE

So graph["start"] is a hash table. You can get all the out-neighbors for Start like this:

```
>>> print(list(graph["start"].keys()))
["a", "b"]
```

There's an edge from Start to A and an edge from Start to B. What if you want to find the weights of those edges?

```
>>> print(graph["start"]["a"])
6
>>> print(graph["start"]["b"])
2
```

Let's add the rest of the nodes and their out-neighbors to the graph:

```
graph["a"] = {}
graph["a"]["fin"] = 1

graph["b"] = {}
graph["b"]["a"] = 3
graph["b"]["fin"] = 5

graph["fin"] = {}        ◄·············    The Finish node doesn't have any out-neighbors.
```

The full graph hash table looks like this.

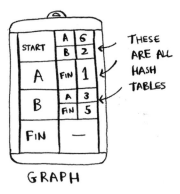

GRAPH

Next, you need a hash table to store the current costs for each node.

COSTS

The *cost* of a node is how long it takes to get to that node from Start. You know it takes 2 minutes from Start to node B. You know it takes 6 minutes to get to node A (although you may find a path that takes less time). You don't know how long it takes to get to Finish. If you don't know the cost yet, you put down infinity. Can you represent *infinity* in Python? Turns out, you can:

```
infinity = math.inf
```

Here's the code to make the costs table:

```
infinity = math.inf
costs = {}
costs["a"] = 6
costs["b"] = 2
costs["fin"] = infinity
```

You also need another hash table for the parents:

PARENTS

Here's the code to make the hash table for the parents:

```
parents = {}
parents["a"] = "start"
parents["b"] = "start"
parents["fin"] = None
```

Finally, you need a set to keep track of all the nodes you've already processed because you don't need to process a node more than once:

```
processed = set()
```

That's all the setup. Now let's look at the algorithm.

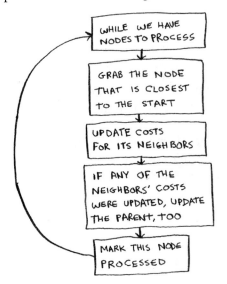

I'll show you the code first and then walk through it. Here's the code:

```
node = find_lowest_cost_node(costs)          ◄············  Finds the lowest-cost
while node is not None:    ◄·······  If you've processed all the        node that you haven't
    cost = costs[node]             nodes, this while loop is done.      processed yet
    neighbors = graph[node]
    for n in neighbors.keys():    ◄·········  Goes through all the out-neighbors of this node
        new_cost = cost + neighbors[n]              If it's cheaper to get to this out-
        if costs[n] > new_cost:   ◄··········  neighbor by going through this node . . .
            costs[n] = new_cost    ◄········  . . . updates the cost for the neighbor
            parents[n] = node   ◄········  This node becomes the new parent for this out-neighbor.
    processed.add(node)    ◄········  Marks the node as processed
    node = find_lowest_cost_node(costs)   ◄········  Finds the next node to process and loops
```

That's Dijkstra's algorithm in Python! Let's see this code in action. Then I'll show you the code for the `find_lowest_cost_node` function.

Find the node with the lowest cost.

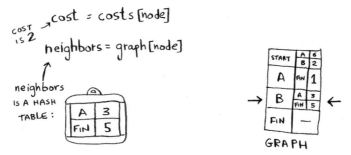

Get the cost and out-neighbors of that node.

Loop through the out-neighbors.

Each node has a cost. The cost is how long it takes to get to that node from Start. Here, you're calculating how long it would take to get to node A if you went Start > node B > node A, instead of Start > node A.

Let's compare those costs.

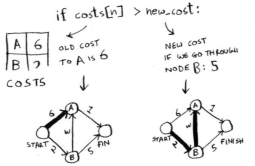

You found a shorter path to node A! Update the cost.

$$costs[n] = new\_cost$$

A	~~8~~ 5	←
B	2	
FIN	∞	

"A"   5

COSTS

The new path goes through node B, so set B as the new parent.

$$parents[n] = node$$

A	~~—~~ B	←
B	START	
FIN	—	

"A"   "B"

PARENTS

OK, you're back at the top of the loop. The next out-neighbor in the `for` loop is the Finish node.

for n in neighbors.keys():

n is "FIN" | A | FIN |

How long does it take to get to Finish if you go through node B?

new_cost = cost + neighbors[n]

2   DISTANCE FROM B TO THE FINISH: 5

} 2 + 5 = 7

It takes 7 minutes. The previous cost was infinity minutes, and 7 minutes is less than that.

if costs[n] > new_cost:

| FIN | ∞ | ←
|---|---|

COSTS   WE HAD NO COST TO THE FINISH BEFORE THIS

7

Set the new cost and the new parent for the Finish node.

$$costs[n] = new\text{-}cost$$

"FIN"   7

A	5
B	2
FIN	~~8~~ 7	←

COSTS

$$parents[n] = node$$

"FIN"   "B"

A	B
B	START
FIN	B	←

PARENTS

OK, you updated the costs for all the out-neighbors of node B. Mark it as processed.

$$processed.append(node)$$

"B"

PROCESSED
NODES: | B |

Find the next node to process.

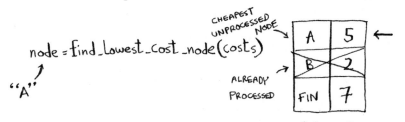

$$node = find\_lowest\_cost\_node(costs)$$

"A"

CHEAPEST UNPROCESSED NODE

ALREADY PROCESSED

| A | 5 | ←
|-----|-----|
| ~~B~~ | ~~2~~ |
| FIN | 7 |

COSTS

Get the cost and out-neighbors for node A.

$$cost = costs[node]$$

5

$$neighbors = graph[node]$$

| FIN | 1 |

Node A only has one out-neighbor: the Finish node.

for n in neighbors.keys():
　　　↗
　"FIN"　　　‿‿‿‿‿‿
　　　　　　　FIN

Currently, it takes 7 minutes to get to the Finish node. How long would it take to get there if you went through node A?

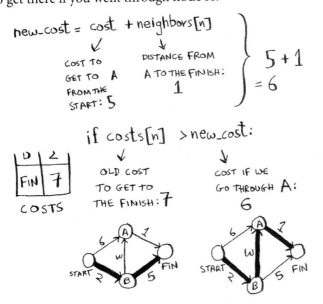

new_cost = cost + neighbors[n]

↓ COST TO GET TO A FROM THE START: 5

↓ DISTANCE FROM A TO THE FINISH: 1

$$5 + 1 = 6$$

if costs[n] > new_cost:

↓ OLD COST TO GET TO THE FINISH: 7

↓ COST IF WE GO THROUGH A: 6

D	2
FIN	7

COSTS

It's faster to get to Finish from node A! Let's update the cost and parent.

costs[n] = new_cost
　↗　　　↗
"FIN"　　6

A	5
B	2
FIN	~~7~~ 6	←

COSTS

parents[n] = node
　↗　　　↗
"FIN"　　"A"

A	B
B	START
FIN	A	←

PARENTS

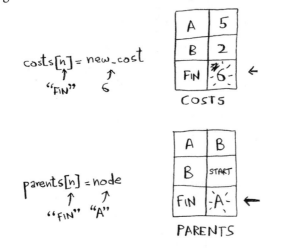

Once you've processed all the nodes, the algorithm is over. I hope the walkthrough helped you understand the algorithm a little better. Finding the lowest-cost node is pretty easy with the `find_lowest_cost_node` function. Here it is in code:

```
def find_lowest_cost_node(costs):
    lowest_cost = math.inf
    lowest_cost_node = None
    for node in costs:         ◄········ Goes through each node
        cost = costs[node]
        if cost < lowest_cost and node not in processed: ◄········
            lowest_cost = cost         ◄······· ...sets it as the new
            lowest_cost_node = node            lowest-cost node
    return lowest_cost_node
```

If it's the lowest cost so far and hasn't been processed yet . . .

To find the lowest cost node, we loop through all the nodes each time. There is a more efficient version of this algorithm. It uses a data structure called a priority queue. A priority queue is itself built on top of a different data structure called a heap. If you're curious about priority queues and heaps, check out the section on heaps in the last chapter of the book.

EXERCISE

9.1 In each of these graphs, what is the weight of the shortest path from Start to Finish?

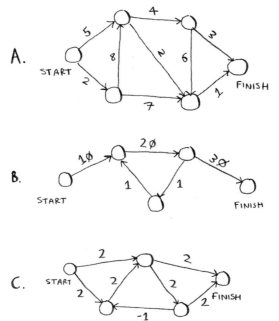

Recap

- Breadth-first search is used to calculate the shortest path for an unweighted graph.

- Dijkstra's algorithm is used to calculate the shortest path for a weighted graph.

- Dijkstra's algorithm works when all the weights are nonnegative.

- If you have negative weights, use the Bellman–Ford algorithm.

greedy algorithms | 10

In this chapter

- You learn about the greedy strategy, a very simple problem-solving strategy.

- You learn how to cope with the impossible: problems that have no fast algorithmic solution (NP-hard problems).

- You learn about approximation algorithms, which you can use to find an approximate solution to an NP-hard problem quickly.

- You learn about the greedy strategy, a very simple problem-solving strategy.

The classroom scheduling problem

Suppose you have a classroom and want to hold as many classes here as possible. You get a list of classes.

CLASS	START	END
ART	9 AM	10 AM
ENG	9:30 AM	10:30 AM
MATH	10 AM	11 AM
CS	10:30 AM	11:30 AM
MUSIC	11 AM	12 PM

You can't hold *all* of these classes in there because some of them overlap.

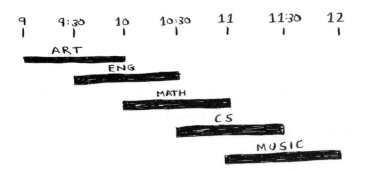

You want to hold as many classes as possible in this classroom. How do you pick what set of classes to hold so that you get the biggest set of classes possible?

Sounds like a hard problem, right? Actually, the algorithm is so easy it might surprise you. Here's how it works:

1. Pick the class that ends the soonest. This is the first class you'll hold in this classroom.

2. Now, you have to pick a class that starts after the first class. Again, pick the class that ends the soonest. This is the second class you'll hold.

Keep doing this, and you'll end up with the answer! Let's try it out. Art ends the soonest, at 10:00 a.m., so that's one of the classes you pick.

ART	9AM	10AM	✓
ENG	4:30AM	10:30AM	
MATH	10AM	11AM	
CS	10:30AM	11:30AM	
MUSIC	11AM	12PM	

Now you need the next class that starts after 10:00 a.m. and ends the soonest.

ART	9AM	10AM	✓
ENG	4:30AM	10:30AM	X
MATH	10AM	11AM	✓
CS	10:30AM	11:30AM	
MUSIC	11AM	12PM	

English is out because it conflicts with Art, but Math works.

Finally, CS conflicts with Math, but Music works.

ART	9AM	10AM	✓
ENG	4:30AM	10:30AM	X
MATH	10AM	11AM	✓
CS	10:30AM	11:30AM	X
MUSIC	11AM	12PM	✓

So these are the three classes you'll hold in this classroom.

A lot of people tell me that this algorithm seems easy. It's too obvious, so it must be wrong. But that's the beauty of greedy algorithms: they're easy! A greedy algorithm is simple: at each step, pick the optimal move. In this case, each time you pick a class, you pick the class that ends the soonest. In technical terms, *at each step, you pick the locally optimal solution*, and in the end, you're left with the globally optimal solution. Believe it or not, this simple algorithm finds the optimal solution to this scheduling problem!

Obviously, greedy algorithms don't always work. But they're simple to write! Let's look at another example.

The knapsack problem

Suppose you're a greedy thief. You're in a store with a knapsack, and there are all these items you can steal. But you can only take what you can fit in your knapsack. The knapsack can hold 35 pounds.

You're trying to maximize the value of the items you put in your knapsack. What algorithm do you use?

Again, the greedy strategy is pretty simple:

1. Pick the most expensive thing that will fit in your knapsack.

2. Pick the next most expensive thing that will fit in your knapsack. And so on.

Except this time, it doesn't work! For example, suppose there are three items you can steal.

STEREO
$3000
30 lbs

LAPTOP
$2000
20 lbs

GUITAR
$1500
15 lbs

Your knapsack can hold 35 pounds of items. The stereo system is the most expensive, so you steal that. Now you don't have space for anything else.

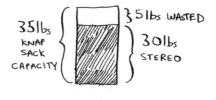

VALUE: $3000

You got $3,000 worth of goods. But wait! If you'd picked the laptop and the guitar instead, you could have had $3,500 worth of loot!

VALUE: $3500

Clearly, the greedy strategy doesn't give you the optimal solution here. Sometimes, it gives poor results. But sometimes, it can get you close. In the next chapter, I'll explain how to calculate the correct solution.

Here's the takeaway from this second example: *sometimes perfect is the enemy of good*. Sometimes all you need is an algorithm that solves the problem pretty well. And that's where greedy algorithms shine because they're simple to write and get results that are often good enough.

EXERCISES

10.1 You work for a furniture company, and you have to ship furniture all over the country. You need to pack your truck with boxes. All the boxes are of different sizes, and you're trying to maximize the space you use in each truck. How would you pick boxes to maximize space? Come up with a greedy strategy. Will that give you the optimal solution?

10.2 You're going to Europe, and you have seven days to see everything you can. You assign a point value to each item (how much you want to see it) and estimate how long it takes. How can you maximize the point total (seeing all the things you really want to see) during your stay? Come up with a greedy strategy. Will that give you the optimal solution?

Let's look at one last example. This is an example where greedy algorithms are absolutely necessary.

The set-covering problem

Suppose you're starting a radio show. You want to reach listeners in all 50 US states. You have to decide what stations to play on to reach all those listeners. It costs money to be on each station, so you're trying to minimize the number of stations you play on. You have a list of stations.

RADIO STATION	AVAILABLE IN
KONE	ID, NV, UT
KTWO	WA, ID, MT
KTHREE	OR, NV, CA
KFOUR	NV, UT
KFIVE	CA, AZ

...etc...

Each station covers a region, and there's overlap.

How do you figure out the smallest set of stations you can play on to cover all 50 states? Sounds easy, doesn't it? Turns out it's extremely hard. Here's how to do it.

List every possible subset of stations. This is called the *power set*. There are 2^n possible subsets.

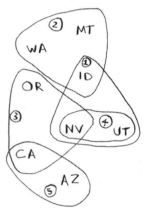

SET #1   ...

SET #8   ...

SET #500

...etc...   ...etc..   ... etc...

From these, pick the set with the smallest number of stations that covers all 50 states.

The problem is that it takes a long time to calculate every possible subset of stations. It takes $O(2^n)$ time because there are 2^n subsets. It's possible to do if you have a small set of 5 to 10 stations. But with all the examples here, think about what will happen if you have a lot of items. It takes much longer if you have more stations. Suppose you can calculate 10 subsets per second.

There's no known algorithm that solves it fast enough! What can you do?

NUMBER OF STATIONS	TIME TAKEN
5	3.2 sec
10	102.4 sec
32	13.6 years
100	4×10^{21} years

Approximation algorithms

Greedy algorithms to the rescue! Here's a greedy algorithm that comes pretty close:

1. Pick the station that covers the most states that haven't been covered yet. It's OK if the station covers some states that have been covered already.

2. Repeat until all the states are covered.

This is called an *approximation algorithm*. When calculating the exact solution will take too much time, an approximation algorithm will work. Approximation algorithms are judged by

• How fast they are

• How close they are to the optimal solution

Greedy algorithms are a good choice because not only are they simple to come up with, but that simplicity means they usually run fast, too. In this case, the greedy algorithm runs in $O(n^2)$ time, where n is the number of radio stations.

Let's see how this problem looks in code.

Code for setup

For this example, I'm going to use a subset of the states and the stations to keep things simple.

First, make a list of the states you want to cover:

```
states_needed = set(["mt", "wa", "or", "id", "nv", "ut",
"ca", "az"])   ◄ ·············   You pass an array in, and it gets converted to a set.
```

I used a set for this. A set is like a list, except that each item can show up only once in a set. *Sets can't have duplicates.* For example, suppose you had this list:

```
>>> arr = [1, 2, 2, 3, 3, 3]
```

And you converted it to a set:

```
>>> set(arr)
set([1, 2, 3])
```

The numbers 1, 2, and 3 all show up just once in a set.

You also need the list of stations that you're choosing from. I chose to use a `dict` for this:

```
stations = {}
stations["kone"] = set(["id", "nv", "ut"])
stations["ktwo"] = set(["wa", "id", "mt"])
stations["kthree"] = set(["or", "nv", "ca"])
stations["kfour"] = set(["nv", "ut"])
stations["kfive"] = set(["ca", "az"])
```

The keys are station names, and the values are the states they cover. So, in this example, the kone station covers Idaho, Nevada, and Utah. All the values are sets, too. Making everything a set will make your life easier, as you'll see soon.

Finally, you need something to hold the final set of stations you'll use:

```
final_stations = set()
```

Calculating the answer

Now you need to calculate what stations you'll use. Take a look at the image at right, and see if you can predict what stations you should use.

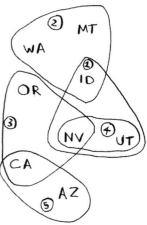

There can be more than one correct solution. You need to go through every station and pick the one that covers the most uncovered states. I'll call this `best_station`:

```
best_station = None
states_covered = set()
for station, states_for_station in stations.items():
```

`states_covered` is the biggest set of states we can newly cover. Remember, we are trying to find the station that will cover the most states that haven't been covered yet. The `for` loop allows you to loop over every station to see which one is the best station. Let's look at the body of the `for` loop:

```
covered = states_needed & states_for_station
if len(covered) > len(states_covered):
   best_station = station
   states_covered = covered
```

⟵······· **New syntax! This is called a set intersection.**

There's a funny-looking line here:

```
covered = states_needed & states_for_station
```

What's going on?

Sets

Suppose you have a set of fruits.

You also have a set of vegetables.

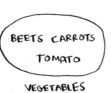

When you have two sets, you can do some fun things with them.

Here are some things you can do with sets.

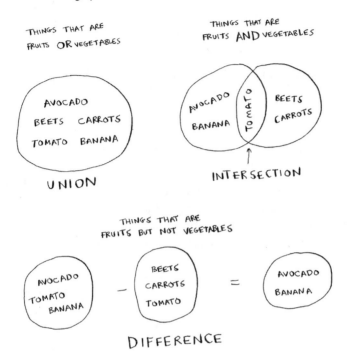

- A set union means "combine both sets."

- A set intersection means "find the items that show up in both sets" (in this case, just the tomato).

- A set difference means "subtract the items in one set from the items in the other set."

For example:

```
>>> fruits = set(["avocado", "tomato", "banana"])
>>> vegetables = set(["beets", "carrots", "tomato"])
>>> fruits | vegetables          This is a set union.
set(["avocado", "beets", "carrots", "tomato", "banana"])
>>> fruits & vegetables          This is a set intersection.
set(["tomato"])
>>> fruits - vegetables          This is a set difference.
set(["avocado", "banana"])
>>> vegetables - fruits          What do you think this will do?
```

To recap:

- Sets are like lists, except sets can't have duplicates.

- You can do some interesting operations on sets, like union, intersection, and difference.

Back to the code

Let's get back to the original example.

This is a set intersection:

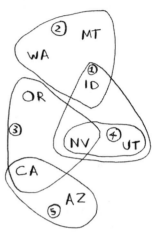

```
covered = states_needed & states_for_station
```

`covered` is a set of states that were in both `states_needed` and `states_for_station`. So `covered` is the set of uncovered states that this station covers! Next you check whether this station covers more states than the current `best_station`:

```
if len(covered) > len(states_covered):
  best_station = station
  states_covered = covered
```

If so, this station is the new `best_station`. Finally, after the `for` loop is over, you add `best_station` to the final list of stations:

```
final_stations.add(best_station)
```

You also need to update `states_needed`. Because this station covers some states, those states aren't needed anymore:

```
states_needed -= states_covered
```

And you loop until `states_needed` is empty. Here's the full code for the loop:

```
while states_needed:
  best_station = None
  states_covered = set()
  for station, states in stations.items():
    covered = states_needed & states
    if len(covered) > len(states_covered):
      best_station = station
      states_covered = covered

  states_needed -= states_covered
  final_stations.add(best_station)
```

Finally, you can print `final_stations`, and you should see this:

```
>>> print(final_stations)
set(['ktwo', 'kthree', 'kone', 'kfive'])
```

Is that what you expected? Instead of stations 1, 2, 3, and 5, you could have chosen stations 2, 3, 4, and 5. Let's compare the run time of the greedy algorithm to the exact algorithm.

NUMBER OF STATIONS	$O(2^n)$ EXACT ALGORITHM	$O(n^2)$ GREEDY ALGORITHM
5	3.2 sec	2.5 sec
10	102.4 sec	10 sec
32	13.6 yrs	102.4 sec
100	4×10^{21} yrs	16.67 min

The greedy algorithm won't always give an exact answer, but it runs much faster. The set-covering problem is known as an NP-hard problem. If you want to learn a little more about NP-hard problems, check out appendix B.

Recap

- Greedy algorithms optimize locally, hoping to end up with a global optimum.

- If you have an NP-hard problem, your best bet is to use an approximation algorithm.

- Greedy algorithms are easy to write and fast to run, so they make good approximation algorithms.

dynamic programming | **11**

....

In this chapter

- You learn dynamic programming, a technique to solve a hard problem by breaking it up into sub-problems and solving those subproblems first.

- Using examples, you learn how to come up with a dynamic programming solution to a new problem.

....

The knapsack problem (revisited)

Let's revisit the knapsack problem from chapter 10. You're a thief with a knapsack that can carry 4 lb of goods.

You have three items that you can put into the knapsack.

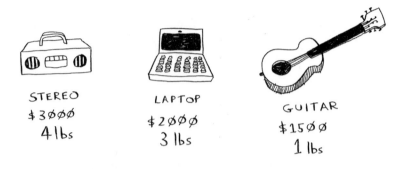

STEREO
$3000
4 lbs

LAPTOP
$2000
3 lbs

GUITAR
$1500
1 lbs

What items should you steal so that you steal the maximum money's worth of goods?

The simple solution

The simplest algorithm is this: you try every possible set of goods and find the set that gives you the most value.

This works, but it's really slow. For 3 items, you have to calculate 8 possible sets. For 4 items, you have to calculate 16 sets. With every item you add, the number of sets you have to calculate doubles! This algorithm takes $O(2^n)$ time, which is very, very slow.

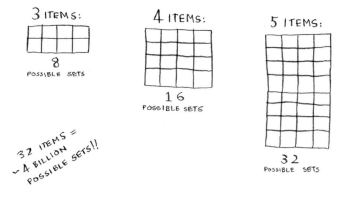

3 ITEMS:

8
POSSIBLE SETS

4 ITEMS:

16
POSSIBLE SETS

5 ITEMS:

32
POSSIBLE SETS

32 ITEMS =
~ 4 BILLION
POSSIBLE SETS!!

That's impractical for any reasonable number of goods. In chapter 10, you saw how to calculate an *approximate* solution. That solution will be close to the optimal solution, but it may not be the optimal solution.

So how do you calculate the optimal solution?

Dynamic programming

Answer: With dynamic programming! Let's see how the dynamic programming algorithm works here. Dynamic programming starts by solving subproblems and builds up to solving the big problem.

For the knapsack problem, you'll start by solving the problem for smaller knapsacks (or sub-knapsacks) and then work up to solving the original problem.

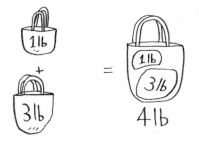

1 lb

+

3 lb

=

1 lb
3 lb

4 lb

Dynamic programming is a hard concept, so don't worry if you don't get it right away. We're going to look at a lot of examples.

I'll start by showing you the algorithm in action. After you've seen it in action once, you'll have a lot of questions! I'll do my best to address every question.

Every dynamic programming algorithm starts with a grid. Here's a grid for the knapsack problem.

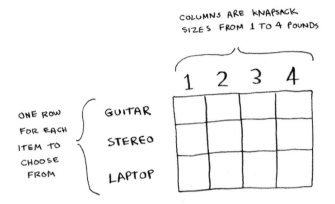

The rows of the grid are the items, and the columns are knapsack weights from 1 lb to 4 lb. You need all of those columns because they will help you calculate the values of the sub-knapsacks.

The grid starts out empty. You're going to fill in each cell of the grid. Once the grid is filled in, you'll have your answer to this problem! Please follow along. Make your own grid, and we'll fill it out together.

The guitar row

I'll show you the exact formula for calculating this grid later. Let's do a walkthrough first. Start with the first row.

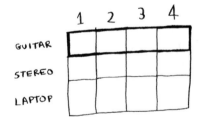

This is the *guitar* row, which means you're trying to fit the guitar into the knapsack. At each cell, there's a simple decision: Do you steal the guitar or not? Remember, you're trying to find the set of items to steal that will give you the most value.

The first cell has a knapsack of capacity 1 lb. The guitar is also 1 lb, which means it fits into the knapsack! So the value of this cell is $1,500, and it contains a guitar.

Let's start filling in the grid.

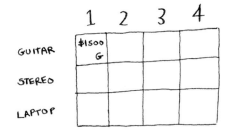

Like this, each cell in the grid will contain a list of all the items that fit into the knapsack at that point.

Let's look at the next cell. Here you have a knapsack with a capacity of 2 lb. Well, the guitar will definitely fit in there!

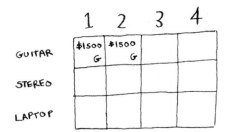

The same is true for the rest of the cells in this row. Remember, this is the first row, so you have *only* the guitar to choose from. You're pretending that the other two items aren't available to steal right now.

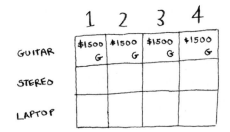

At this point, you're probably confused. *Why* are you doing this for knapsacks with a capacity of 1 lb, 2 lb, and so on, when the problem talks about a 4 lb knapsack? Remember how I told you that dynamic programming starts with a small problem and builds up to the big problem? You're solving subproblems here that will help you to solve the big problem. Read on, and things will become clearer.

At this point, your grid should look like this.

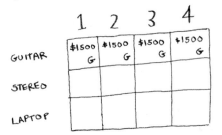

Remember, you're trying to maximize the value of the knapsack. *This row represents the current best guess for this max.* So right now, according to this row, if you had a knapsack of capacity 4 lb, the max value you could put in there would be $1,500.

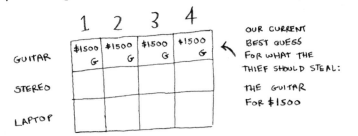

You know that's not the final solution. As we go through the algorithm, you'll refine your estimate.

The stereo row

Let's do the next row. This one is for the stereo. Now that you're on the second row, you can steal the stereo or the guitar. At every row, you can steal the item at that row or the items in the rows above it. So you can't choose to steal the laptop right now, but you can steal the stereo and/or the guitar. Let's start with the first cell, a knapsack of capacity 1 lb. The current max value you can fit into a knapsack of 1 lb is $1,500.

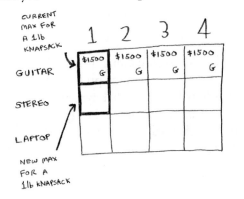

Should you steal the stereo or not?

You have a knapsack of capacity 1 lb. Will the stereo fit in there? Nope, it's too heavy! Because you can't fit the stereo, $1,500 *remains* the max guess for a 1 lb knapsack.

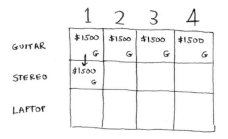

The same thing is true for the next two cells. These knapsacks have a capacity of 2 lb and 3 lb. The old max value for both was $1,500.

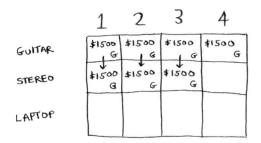

The stereo still doesn't fit, so your guesses remain unchanged.

What if you have a knapsack of capacity 4 lb? Aha! The stereo finally fits! The old max value was $1,500, but if you put the stereo in there instead, the value is $3,000! Let's take the stereo.

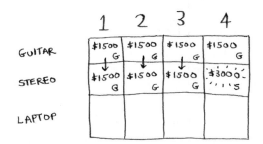

You just updated your estimate! If you have a 4 lb knapsack, you can fit at least $3,000 worth of goods in it. You can see from the grid that you're incrementally updating your estimate.

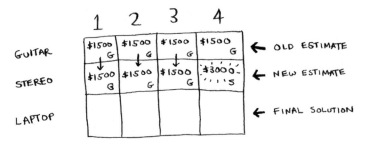

The laptop row

Let's do the same thing with the laptop! The laptop weighs 3 lb, so it won't fit into a 1 lb or a 2 lb knapsack. The estimate for the first two cells stays at $1,500.

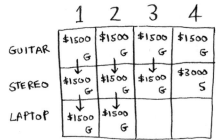

At 3 lb, the old estimate was $1,500. But you can choose the laptop instead, and that's worth $2,000. So the new max estimate is $2,000!

At 4 lb, things get really interesting. This is an important part. The current estimate is $3,000. You can put the laptop in the knapsack, but it's only worth $2,000.

Hmm, that's not as good as the old estimate. But wait! The laptop weighs only 3 lb, so you have 1 lb free! You could put something in this 1 lb.

What's the maximum value you can fit into 1 lb of space? Well, you've been calculating it all along.

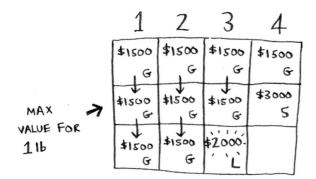

According to the last best estimate, you can fit the guitar into that 1 lb space, and that's worth $1,500. So the real comparison is as follows.

$$\$3000 \text{ vs } \left(\$2000 + \$1500\right)$$
$$\text{STEREO} \quad \text{LAPTOP} \quad \text{GUITAR}$$

You might have been wondering why you were calculating max values for smaller knapsacks. I hope now it makes sense! When you have space left over, you can use the answers to those subproblems to figure out what will fit in that space. It's better to take the laptop + the guitar for $3,500.

The final grid looks like this.

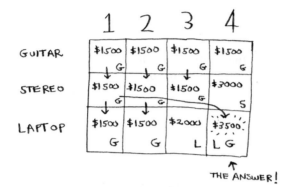

There's the answer: the maximum value that will fit in the knapsack is $3,500, made up of a guitar and a laptop!

Maybe you think I used a different formula to calculate the value of that last cell. That's because I skipped some unnecessary complexity when filling in the values of the earlier cells. Each cell's value gets calculated with the same formula. Here it is.

$$\text{CELL}[i][j] = \max \text{ of} \begin{cases} \text{1. THE PREVIOUS MAX (VALUE AT CELL } [i-1][j]) \\ \qquad\qquad\qquad vs \\ \text{2. VALUE OF CURRENT ITEM + VALUE OF THE REMAINING SPACE} \\ \qquad\qquad\qquad\qquad\qquad \text{CELL}[i-1][j - \text{ITEM'S WEIGHT}] \end{cases}$$

ROW   COLUMN

You can use this formula with every cell in this grid, and you should end up with the same grid I did. Remember how I talked about solving subproblems? You combined the solutions to two subproblems to solve the bigger problem.

Knapsack problem FAQ

Maybe this still feels like magic. This section answers some common questions.

What happens if you add an item?

Suppose you realize there's a fourth item you can steal that you didn't notice before! You can also steal an iPhone.

IPHONE
$2000
1lb

Do you have to recalculate everything to account for this new item? Nope. Remember, dynamic programming keeps progressively building on your estimate. So far, these are the max values.

	1	2	3	4
GUITAR	$1500 G	$1500 G	$1500 G	$1500 G
STEREO	$1500 G	$1500 G	$1500 G	$3000 S
LAPTOP	$1500 G	$1500 G	$2000 L	$3500 LG

That means for a 4 lb knapsack, you can steal $3,500 worth of goods. You thought that was the final max value. But let's add a row for the iPhone.

	1	2	3	4
GUITAR	$1500 G	$1500 G	$1500 G	$1500 G
STEREO	$1500 G	$1500 G	$1500 G	$3000 S
LAPTOP	$1500 G	$1500 G	$2000 L	$3500 LG
IPHONE				

NEW ANSWER

Turns out you have a new max value! Try to fill in this new row before reading on.

Let's start with the first cell. The iPhone fits into the 1 lb knapsack. The old max was $1,500, but the iPhone is worth $2,000. Let's take the iPhone instead.

	1	2	3	4
GUITAR	$1500 G	$1500 G	$1500 G	$1500 G
STEREO	$1500 G	$1500 G	$1500 G	$3000 S
LAPTOP	$1500 G	$1500 G	$2000 L	$3500 LG
IPHONE	$2000 I			

In the next cell, you can fit the iPhone *and* the guitar.

$1500 G	$1500 G	$1500 G	$1500 G
$1500 G	$1500 G	$1500 G	$3000 S
$1500 G	$1500 G	$2000 L	$3500 LG
$2000 I	$3500 IG		

For cell 3, you can't do better than take the iPhone and the guitar again, so leave it as is.

For the last cell, things get interesting. The current max is $3,500. You can steal the iPhone instead, and you have 3 lb of space left over.

$$\$3500 \quad \text{vs} \left(\underset{\text{IPHONE}}{\$2000} + \underset{\text{3 LBS FREE}}{???} \right)$$

LAPTOP + GUITAR

Those 3 lb are worth $2,000! $2,000 from the iPhone + $2,000 from the old subproblem: that's $4,000. A new max!

Here's the new final grid.

$1500 G	$1500 G	$1500 G	$1500 G
$1500 G	$1500 G	$1500 G	$3000 S
$1500 G	$1500 G	$2000 L	$3500 LG
$2000 I	$3500 IG	$3500 IG	$4000 IL

↑
NEW
ANSWER

Question: Would the value of a column ever go *down*? Is this possible?

	1	2	3	4
MAX VALUE DECREASED AS WE WENT ON	$1500	$1500	$1500	$1500
	Ø	Ø	Ø	$3000

Think of an answer before reading on.

Answer: No. At every iteration, you're storing the current max estimate. The estimate can never get worse than it was before!

EXERCISE

11.1 Suppose you can steal another item: a mechanical keyboard player. It weighs 1 lb and is worth $1,000. Should you steal it?

What happens if you change the order of the rows?

Does the answer change? Suppose you fill the rows in this order: stereo, laptop, guitar. What does the grid look like? Fill out the grid for yourself before moving on.

Here's what the grid looks like.

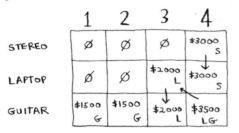

The answer doesn't change. The order of the rows doesn't matter.

Can you fill in the grid column-wise instead of row-wise?

Try it for yourself! For this problem, it doesn't make a difference. It could make a difference for other problems.

What happens if you add a smaller item?

Suppose you can steal a necklace. It weighs 0.5 lb, and it's worth $1,000. So far, your grid assumes that all weights are integers. Now you decide to steal the necklace. You have 3.5 lb left over. What's the max value you can fit in 3.5 lb? You don't know! You only calculated values for 1 lb, 2 lb, 3 lb, and 4 lb knapsacks. You need to know the value of a 3.5 lb knapsack.

Because of the necklace, you have to account for finer granularity, so the grid has to change.

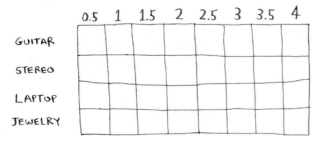

Can you steal fractions of an item?

Suppose you're a thief in a grocery store. You can steal bags of lentils and rice. If a whole bag doesn't fit, you can open it and take as much as you can carry. So now it's not all or nothing—you can take a fraction of an item. How do you handle this using dynamic programming?

Answer: You can't. With the dynamic programming solution, you either take the item or not. There's no way for it to figure out that you should take half an item.

But this case is easily solved using a greedy algorithm! First, take as much as you can of the most valuable item. When that runs out, take as much as you can of the next most valuable item, and so on.

For example, suppose you have these items to choose from.

QUINOA   DAL   RICE
$6/lb $3/lb $2/lb

Quinoa is more expensive per pound than anything else. So, take all the quinoa you can carry! If that fills your knapsack, that's the best you can do.

KNAPSACK
FULL OF
QUINOA

If the quinoa runs out and you still have space in your knapsack, take the next most valuable item, and so on.

Optimizing your travel itinerary

Suppose you're going to London for a nice vacation. You have two days there and a lot of things you want to do. You can't do everything, so you make a list.

ATTRACTION	TIME	RATING
WESTMINSTER ABBEY	½ DAY	7
GLOBE THEATER	½ DAY	6
NATIONAL GALLERY	1 DAY	9
BRITISH MUSEUM	2 DAYS	9
ST. PAUL'S CATHEDRAL	½ DAY	8

For each thing you want to see, you write down how long it will take and rate how much you want to see it. Can you figure out what you should visit based on this list?

It's the knapsack problem again! Instead of a knapsack, you have a limited amount of time. And instead of stereos and laptops, you have a list of places you want to go. Draw the dynamic programming grid for this list before moving on.

Here's what the grid looks like.

	½	1	1½	2
WESTMINSTER				
GLOBE THEATER				
NATIONAL GALLERY				
BRITISH MUSEUM				
ST. PAUL'S				

Did you get it right? Fill in the grid. What places should you end up visiting? Here's the answer.

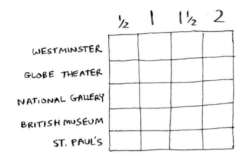

	½	1	1½	2
WESTMINSTER	7 W	7 W	7 W	7 W
GLOBE THEATER	7 W	13 WG	13 WG	13 WG
NATIONAL GALLERY	7 W	13 WG	16 WN	22 WGN
BRITISH MUSEUM	7 W	13 WG	16 WN	22 WGN
ST PAUL'S	8 S	15 WS	21 WGS	24 WNS

FINAL ANSWER:
WESTMINSTER ABBEY,
NATIONAL GALLERY,
ST. PAUL'S CATHEDRAL

Handling items that depend on each other

Suppose you want to go to Paris, so you add a couple of items to the list.

EIFFEL TOWER	1½ DAY	8
THE LOUVRE	1½ DAY	9
NOTRE DAME	1½ DAY	7

These places take a lot of time because first you have to travel from London to Paris. That takes half a day. If you want to do all three items, it will take 4.5 days.

Wait, that's not right. You don't have to travel to Paris for each item. Once you're in Paris, each item should only take a day. So it should be one day per item + half a day of travel = 3.5 days, not 4.5 days.

If you put the Eiffel Tower in your knapsack, the Louvre becomes "cheaper"—it will only cost you a day instead of 1.5 days. How do you model this in dynamic programming?

You can't. Dynamic programming is powerful because it can solve subproblems and use those answers to solve the big problem. *Dynamic programming only works when each subproblem is discrete—when it doesn't depend on other subproblems.* That means there's no way to account for Paris using the dynamic programming algorithm.

Is it possible that the solution will require more than two sub-knapsacks?

It's possible that the best solution involves stealing more than two items. The way the algorithm is set up, you're combining two knapsacks at most—you'll never have more than two sub-knapsacks. But it's possible for those sub-knapsacks to have their own sub-knapsacks.

IT'S NOT POSSIBLE TO HAVE THREE SUB-KNAPSACKS

BUT IT IS POSSIBLE TO HAVE SUB-KNAPSACKS THAT HAVE THEIR OWN SUB-KNAPSACKS

Is it possible that the best solution doesn't fill the knapsack completely?

Yes. Suppose you could also steal a diamond.

This is a big diamond: it weighs 3.5 pounds. It's worth a million dollars, way more than anything else. You should definitely steal it! But there's half a pound of space left, and nothing will fit in that space.

DIAMOND
$1 MILLION
3.5 lbs

EXERCISE

11.2 Suppose you're going camping. You have a knapsack that will hold 6 lb, and you can take the following items. Each has a value, and the higher the value, the more important the item is:

- Water, 3 lb, 10

- Book, 1 lb, 3

- Food, 2 lb, 9

- Jacket, 2 lb, 5

- Camera, 1 lb, 6

What's the optimal set of items to take on your camping trip?

Longest common substring

You've seen one dynamic programming problem so far. What are the takeaways?

- Dynamic programming is useful *when you're trying to optimize something given a constraint*. In the knapsack problem, you had to maximize the value of the goods you stole, constrained by the size of the knapsack.

- You can use dynamic programming when the problem can be broken into discrete subproblems, and they don't depend on each other.

It can be hard to come up with a dynamic programming solution. That's what we'll focus on in this section. Some general tips follow:

- It's often useful to picture a dynamic programming problem as a grid.

- The values in the cells are usually what you're trying to optimize. For the knapsack problem, the values are the value of the goods.

- Each cell is a subproblem, so think about how you can divide your problem into subproblems. That will help you figure out what the axes are.

Let's look at another example. Suppose you're running dictionary.com. Someone types in a word, and you give them the definition.

But if someone misspells a word, you want to be able to guess what word they meant. Alex is searching for *fish*, but he accidentally put in *hish*. That's not a word in your dictionary, but you have a list of words that are similar.

SIMILAR TO "HISH":

- FISH

- VISTA

(This is a toy example, so you'll limit your list to two words. In reality, this list would probably be thousands of words.)

Alex typed *hish*. Which word did Alex mean to type: *fish* or *vista*?

Making the grid

What does the grid for this problem look like? You need to answer these questions:

- What are the values of the cells?

- How do you divide this problem into subproblems?

- What are the axes of the grid?

In dynamic programming, you're trying to *maximize* something. In this case, you're trying to find the longest substring that two words have in common. What substring do *hish* and *fish* have in common? How about *hish* and *vista*? That's what you want to calculate.

Remember, the values for the cells are usually what you're trying to optimize. In this case, the values will probably be a number: the length of the longest substring that the two strings have in common.

How do you divide this problem into subproblems? You could compare substrings. Instead of comparing *hish* and *fish*, you could compare *his* and *fis* first. Each cell will contain the length of the longest substring that two substrings have in common. This also gives you a clue that the axes will probably be the two words. So the grid probably looks like this.

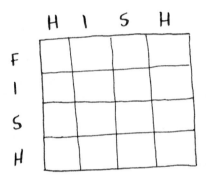

If this seems like black magic to you, don't worry. This is hard stuff—that's why I'm teaching it so late in the book! Later, I'll give you an exercise so you can practice dynamic programming yourself.

Filling in the grid

Now you have a good idea of what the grid should look like. What's the formula for filling in each cell of the grid? You can cheat a little because you already know what the solution should be—*hish* and *fish* have a substring of length 3 in common: *ish*.

But that still doesn't tell you the formula to use. Computer scientists sometimes joke about using the Feynman algorithm. The *Feynman algorithm* is named after the famous physicist Richard Feynman, and it works like this:

1. Write down the problem.

2. Think real hard.

3. Write down the solution.

Computer scientists are a fun bunch!

The truth is that there's no easy way to calculate the formula here. You have to experiment and try to find something that works. Sometimes algorithms aren't an exact recipe. They're a framework that you build your idea on top of.

Try to come up with a solution to this problem yourself. I'll give you a hint—part of the grid looks like this.

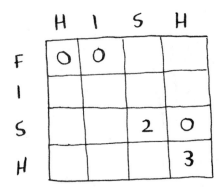

What are the other values? Remember that each cell is the value of a *subproblem*. Why does cell (3, 3) have a value of 2? Why does cell (3, 4) have a value of 0?

Read on after you've tried to come up with a formula yourself. Even if you don't get it right, my explanation will make a lot more sense.

The solution

Here's the final grid.

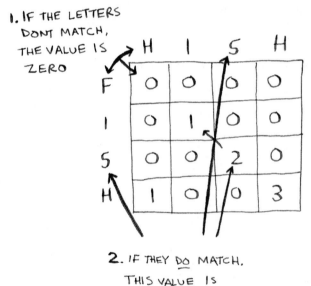

Here's my formula for filling in each cell.

1. IF THE LETTERS DON'T MATCH, THE VALUE IS ZERO

2. IF THEY DO MATCH, THIS VALUE IS VALUE OF TOP-LEFT NEIGHBOR +1

Here's how the formula looks in pseudocode:

```
if word_a[i] == word_b[j]:          The letters match.
   cell[i][j] = cell[i-1][j-1] + 1
else:                               The letters don't match.
   cell[i][j] = 0
```

Here's the grid for *hish vs. vista*.

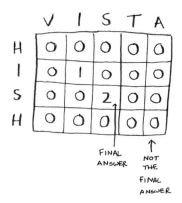

One thing to note: for this problem, the final solution may not be in the last cell! For the knapsack problem, this last cell always had the final solution. But for the longest common substring, the solution is the largest number in the grid—and it may not be the last cell.

Let's go back to the original question: Which string has more in common with *hish*? *hish* and *fish* have a substring of three letters in common. *hish* and *vista* have a substring of two letters in common.

Alex probably meant to type *fish*.

Longest common subsequence

Suppose Alex accidentally searched for *fosh*. Which word did he mean: *fish* or *fort*?

Let's compare them using the longest-common-substring formula.

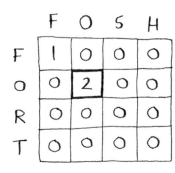 VS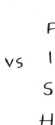

They're both the same: two letters! But *fosh* is closer to *fish*.

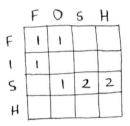

You're comparing the longest common *substring*, but you really need to compare the longest common *subsequence*: the number of letters in a sequence that the two words have in common. How do you calculate the longest common subsequence?

Here's the partial grid for *fish* and *fosh*.

Can you figure out the formula for this grid? The longest common subsequence is very similar to the longest common substring, and the formulas are pretty similar, too. Try to solve it yourself—I give the answer next.

Longest common subsequence—solution

Here's the final grid.

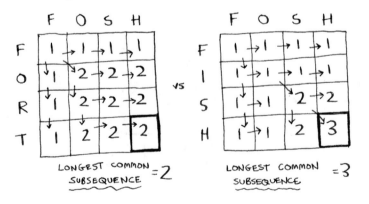

Here's my formula for filling in each cell.

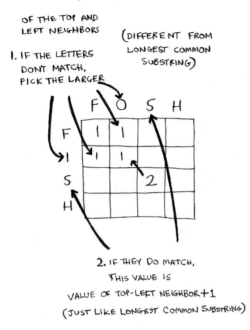

And here it is in pseudocode:

```
if word_a[i] == word_b[j]:                    ◀············ The letters match.
  cell[i][j] = cell[i-1][j-1] + 1
else:                                          ◀············ The letters don't match.
  cell[i][j] = max(cell[i-1][j], cell[i][j-1])
```

Whew! You did it! This is definitely one of the toughest chapters in the book. So is dynamic programming ever really used? The answer is *yes*:

- Biologists use the longest common subsequence to find similarities in DNA strands. They can use this to tell how similar two animals or two diseases are. The longest common subsequence is being used to find a cure for multiple sclerosis.

- Have you ever used `diff` (like `git diff`)? `Diff` tells you the differences between two files, and it uses dynamic programming to do so.

- We talked about string similarity. *Levenshtein distance* measures how similar two strings are, and it uses dynamic programming. Levenshtein distance is used for everything from spell-check to figuring out whether a user is uploading copyrighted data.

EXERCISE

11.3 Draw and fill in the grid to calculate the longest common
substring between *blue* and *clues*.

Recap

- Dynamic programming is useful when you're trying to optimize
  something given a constraint.

- You can use dynamic programming when the problem can be broken
  into discrete subproblems.

- Every dynamic programming solution involves a grid.

- The values in the cells are usually what you're trying to optimize.

- Each cell is a subproblem, so think about how you can divide your
  problem into subproblems.

- There's no single formula for calculating a dynamic programming
  solution.

In this chapter

- You learn to build a classification system using the k-nearest neighbors algorithm.

- You learn about feature extraction.

- You learn about regression: predicting a number, like the value of a stock tomorrow or how much a user will enjoy a movie.

- You learn about the use cases and limitations of k-nearest neighbors.

Classifying oranges vs. grapefruit

Look at this fruit. Is it an orange or a grapefruit? Well, I know that grapefruits are generally bigger and redder.

My thought process is something like this: I have a graph in my mind.

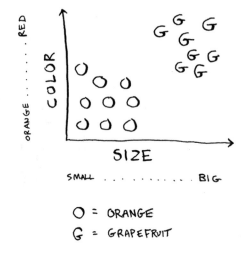

O = ORANGE

G = GRAPEFRUIT

Generally speaking, the bigger, redder fruit are grapefruits. This fruit is big and red, so it's probably a grapefruit. But what if you get a fruit like this?

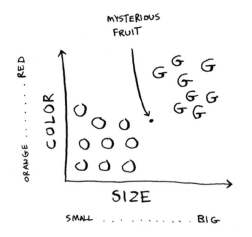

How would you *classify* this fruit? One way is to look at the neighbors of this spot. Take a look at the three closest neighbors of this spot.

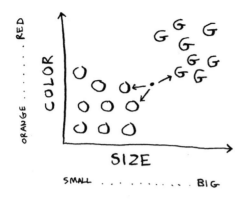

More neighbors are oranges than grapefruit. So this fruit is probably an orange. Congratulations! You just used the *k-nearest neighbors* (KNN) algorithm for *classification*! The whole algorithm is pretty simple.

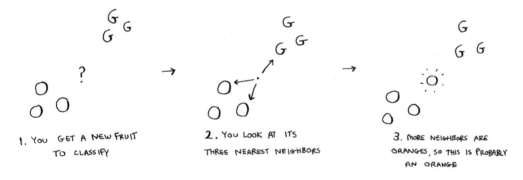

1. YOU GET A NEW FRUIT TO CLASSIFY

2. YOU LOOK AT ITS THREE NEAREST NEIGHBORS

3. MORE NEIGHBORS ARE ORANGES, SO THIS IS PROBABLY AN ORANGE

The KNN algorithm is simple but useful! If you're trying to classify something, you might want to try KNN first. Let's look at a more real-world example.

Building a recommendations system

Suppose you're Netflix, and you want to build a movie recommendations system for your users. On a high level, this is similar to the grapefruit problem!

You can plot every user on a graph.

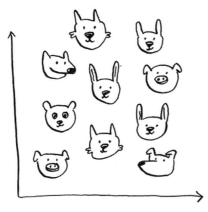

These users are plotted by similarity, so users with similar taste are plotted closer together. Suppose you want to recommend movies for Priyanka. Find the five users closest to her.

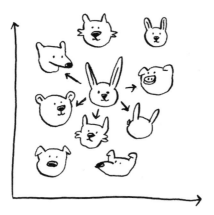

Justin, JC, Joey, Lance, and Chris all have similar taste in movies. So whatever movies *they* like, Priyanka will probably like too!

Once you have this graph, building a recommendations system is easy. If Justin likes a movie, recommend it to Priyanka.

1. JUSTIN WATCHES
   A MOVIE

☆☆☆☆☆
PITCH PERFECT

2. HE LIKES IT

YOU MIGHT LIKE:

PITCH RFECT

3. RECOMMEND IT
   TO PRIYANKA

But there's still a big piece missing. You graphed the users by similarity. How do you figure out how similar two users are?

Feature extraction

In the grapefruit example, you compared fruit based on how big they are and how red they are. Size and color are the *features* you're comparing. Now suppose you have three fruit. You can extract the features.

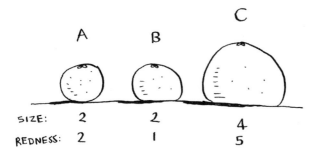

Then you can graph the three fruit.

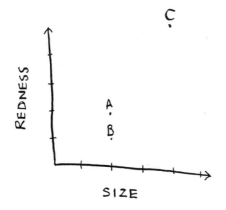

From the graph, you can tell visually that fruits A and B are similar. Let's measure how close they are. To find the distance between two points, you use the Pythagorean formula.

$$\sqrt{(x_1 - x_2)^2 + (y_1 - y_2)^2}$$

Here's the distance between A and B, for example.

$$\sqrt{(2-2)^2 + (2-1)^2}$$

$$= \sqrt{0 + 1}$$

$$= \sqrt{1}$$

$$= 1$$

The distance between A and B is 1. You can find the rest of the distances, too.

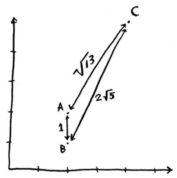

The distance formula confirms what you saw visually: fruits A and B are similar.

Suppose you're comparing Netflix users instead. You need some way to graph the users. So, you need to convert each user to a set of coordinates, just as you did for fruit.

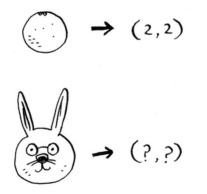

Once you can graph users, you can measure the distance between them.

Here's how you can convert users into a set of numbers. When users sign up for Netflix, have them rate some categories of movies based on how much they like those categories. For each user, you now have a set of ratings!

	PRIYANKA	JUSTIN	MORPHEUS
COMEDY	3	4	2
ACTION	4	3	5
DRAMA	4	5	1
HORROR	1	1	3
ROMANCE	4	5	1

Priyanka and Justin like Romance and hate Horror. Morpheus likes Action but hates Romance (he hates it when a good action movie gets ruined by a cheesy romantic scene). Remember how, in oranges versus grapefruit, each fruit was represented by a set of two numbers? Here, each user is represented by a set of five numbers.

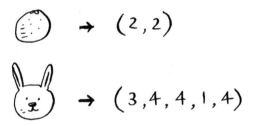

A mathematician would say instead of calculating the distance in two dimensions, you're now calculating the distance in *five* dimensions. But the distance formula remains the same.

$$\sqrt{(a_1-a_2)^2+(b_1-b_2)^2+(c_1-c_2)^2+(d_1-d_2)^2+(e_1-e_2)^2}$$

It just involves a set of five numbers instead of a set of two numbers.

The distance formula is flexible: you could have a set of a *million* numbers and still use the same old distance formula to find the distance. Maybe you're wondering, "What does *distance* mean when you have five numbers?" The distance tells you how similar those sets of numbers are.

$$\sqrt{(3-4)^2+(4-3)^2+(4-5)^2+(1-1)^2+(4-5)^2}$$

$$=\sqrt{1+1+1+0+1}$$

$$=\sqrt{4}$$

$$=2$$

Here's the distance between Priyanka and Justin.

> **Note**
>
> By the way, here's a bit of terminology you'll see often. Those arrays of numbers like (2, 2) for the grapefruit or (3, 4, 4, 1, 4) for Priyanka's taste in movies are called *vectors*. So if you're reading a paper on machine learning, and you see the authors talking about vectors, they mean an array of numbers like that.

Priyanka and Justin are pretty similar. What's the difference between Priyanka and Morpheus? Calculate the distance before moving on.

Did you get it right? Priyanka and Morpheus $\sqrt{24}$ are apart. The distance tells you that Priyanka's tastes are more like Justin's than Morpheus's.

Great! Now recommending movies to Priyanka is easy: if Justin likes a movie, recommend it to Priyanka, and vice versa. You just built a movie recommendations system!

If you're a Netflix user, Netflix will keep telling you, "Please rate more movies. The more movies you rate, the better your recommendations will be." Now you know why. The more movies you rate, the more accurately Netflix can see what other users you're similar to.

EXERCISES

12.1 In the Netflix example, you calculated the distance between two different users using the distance formula. But not all users rate movies the same way. Suppose you have two users, Yogi and Pinky, who have the same taste in movies. But Yogi rates any movie he likes as a 5, whereas Pinky is choosier and reserves the 5s for only the best. They're well matched, but according to the distance algorithm, they aren't neighbors. How would you take their different rating strategies into account?

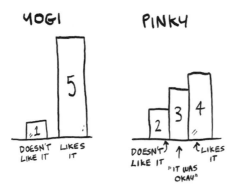

12.2 Suppose Netflix nominates a group of "influencers." For example, Quentin Tarantino and Wes Anderson are influencers on Netflix, so their ratings count for more than a normal user's. How would you change the recommendations system so it's biased toward the ratings of influencers?

Regression

Suppose you want to do more than just recommend a movie: you want to guess how Priyanka will rate this movie. Take the five people closest to her.

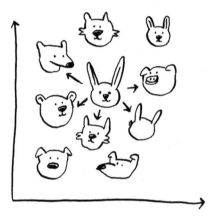

By the way, I keep talking about the closest five people. There's nothing special about the number 5: you could do the closest 2, or 10, or 10,000. That's why the algorithm is called k-nearest neighbors and not five-nearest neighbors!

Suppose you're trying to guess a rating for *Pitch Perfect*. Well, how did Justin, JC, Joey, Lance, and Chris rate it?

JUSTIN : 5

JC : 4

JOEY : 4

LANCE : 5

CHRIS : 3

You could take the average of their ratings and get 4.2 stars. That's called *regression*. These are the two basic things you'll do with KNN— classification and regression:

- Classification = categorization into a group

- Regression = predicting a response (like a number)

Regression is very useful. Suppose you run a small bakery in Berkeley, and you make fresh bread every day. You're trying to predict how many loaves to make for today. You have a set of features:

- Weather on a scale of 1 to 5 (1 = bad, 5 = great).

- Weekend or holiday? (1 if it's a weekend or a holiday, 0 otherwise.)

- Is there a game on? (1 if yes, 0 if no.)

And you know how many loaves of bread you've sold in the past for different sets of features.

A. $(5, 1, 0) = 300$ LOAVES B. $(3, 1, 1) = 225$ LOAVES

C. $(1, 1, 0) = 75$ LOAVES D. $(4, 0, 1) = 200$ LOAVES

E. $(4, 0, 0) = 150$ LOAVES F. $(2, 0, 0) = 50$ LOAVES

Today is a weekend day with good weather. Based on the data you just saw, how many loaves will you sell? Let's use KNN, where k = 4. First, figure out the four nearest neighbors for this point.

$$(4, 1, 0) = ?$$

Here are the distances. A, B, D, and E are the closest.

A. 1 ←

B. 2 ←

C. 9

D. 2 ←

E. 1 ←

F. 5

Take an average of the loaves sold on those days, and you get 218.75. That's how many loaves you should make for today!

Cosine similarity

So far, you've been using the distance formula to compare the distance between two users. Is this the best formula to use? A common one used in practice is *cosine similarity*. Suppose two users are similar, but one is more conservative in their ratings. They both loved Manmohan Desai's *Amar Akbar Anthony*. Paul rated it 5 stars, but Rowan rated it 4 stars. If you keep using the distance formula, these two users might not be each other's neighbors, even though they have similar taste.

Cosine similarity doesn't measure the distance between two vectors. Instead, it compares the angles of the two vectors. It's better at dealing with cases like this. Cosine similarity is out of the scope of this book, but look it up if you use KNN!

Picking good features

To figure out recommendations, you had users rate categories of movies. What if you had them rate pictures of cats instead? Then you'd find users who rated those pictures similarly. This would probably be a worse recommendations engine because the "features" don't have a lot to do with taste in movies!

Or suppose you ask users to rate movies so you can give them recommendations, but you only ask them to rate *Toy Story*, *Toy Story 2*, and *Toy Story 3*. This won't tell you a lot about the users' movie tastes!

When you're working with KNN, it's really important to pick the right features to compare against. Picking the right features means

- Features that directly correlate to the movies you're trying to recommend

- Features that don't have a bias (for example, if you ask the users to only rate comedy movies, that doesn't tell you whether they like action movies)

Do you think ratings are a good way to recommend movies? Maybe I rated *Inception* more highly than *Legally Blonde*, but I actually spend more time watching *Legally Blonde*. How would you improve this Netflix recommendations system?

Going back to the bakery: Can you think of two good and two bad features you could have picked for the bakery? Maybe you need to make more loaves after you advertise in the paper. Or maybe you need to make more loaves on Mondays.

There's no one right answer when it comes to picking good features. You have to think about all the different things you need to consider.

EXERCISE

12.3 Netflix has millions of users. The earlier example looked at the five closest neighbors for building the recommendations system. Is this too low? Too high?

Introduction to machine learning

KNN is a really useful algorithm, and it's your introduction to the magical world of machine learning! Machine learning is all about making your computer more intelligent. You already saw one example of machine learning: building a recommendations system. Let's look at some other examples.

OCR

OCR stands for *optical character recognition*. It means you can take a photo of a page of text, and your computer will automatically read the text for you. Google uses OCR to digitize books. How does OCR work? For example, consider this number.

7

How would you automatically figure out what number this is? You can use KNN for this:

1.   Go through a lot of images of numbers and extract features of those numbers.

2.   When you get a new image, extract the features of that image and see what its nearest neighbors are!

It's the same problem as oranges versus grapefruit. Generally speaking, OCR algorithms measure lines, points, and curves.

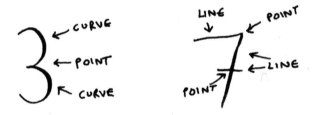

Then, when you get a new character, you can extract the same features from it.

Feature extraction is a lot more complicated in OCR than the fruit example. But it's important to understand that even complex technologies build on simple ideas, like KNN. You could use the same ideas for speech recognition or face recognition. When you upload a photo to Facebook, sometimes it's smart enough to tag people in the photo automatically. That's machine learning in action!

The first step of OCR, where you go through images of numbers and extract features, is called—wait for it—*feature extraction*. This is where you transform the images into something that your machine learning algorithm can work with. The next step is called *training*, where you train a model on your features so it can recognize numbers in images. Most machine-learning algorithms have a training step: before your computer can do the task, it must be trained. The next example involves spam filters, and it has a training step.

Building a spam filter

Spam filters use another simple algorithm called the *Naive Bayes classifier*. First, you train your Naive Bayes classifier on some data.

SUBJECT	SPAM?
"RESET YOUR PASSWORD"	NOT SPAM
"YOU HAVE WON 1 MILLION DOLLARS"	SPAM
"SEND ME YOUR PASSWORD"	SPAM
"HAPPY BIRTHDAY"	NOT SPAM

Suppose you get an email with the subject "Collect your million dollars now!" Is it spam? You can break this sentence into words. Then, for each word, see what the probability is for that word to show up in a spam email. For example, in this very simple model, the word *million* only appears in spam emails. Naive Bayes figures out the probability that something is likely to be spam. It has applications similar to KNN. For example, you could use Naive Bayes to categorize fruit: you have a fruit that's big and red. What's the probability that it's a grapefruit? It's another simple algorithm that's fairly effective. We love those algorithms!

Predicting the stock market

Here's something that's hard to do with machine learning: predicting whether the stock market will go up or down. How do you pick good features in a stock market? Suppose you say that if the stock went up yesterday, it will go up today. Is that a good feature? Or suppose you say that the stock will always go down in May. Will that work? There's no guaranteed way to use past numbers to predict future performance. Predicting the future is hard, and it's almost impossible when there are so many variables involved.

A high-level overview of training an ML model

Now that we've seen a few examples, let's look at the steps to training an ML model. First gather the data. In the Netflix example, our data was movie ratings from users. Then you need to clean the data. Cleaning means getting rid of bad data. For example, you may have users who don't like being prompted to rate movies, so they rate movies randomly and move to the next screen. You will want to remove this data from your data set. You will then need to extract features from your data.

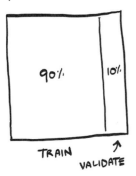

After you have your features, it's time to train your model. Select a model like KNN, SVM's, or a neural network and train it with 90% of your data. Keep the remaining 10% to validate the model. After your model is trained, you will test it by asking it to make a prediction. You can use that 10% of data to see how good that prediction is.

For example, let's say we want to test the Netflix recommendations model. We can ask it how Priyanka would like these movies and shows:

Our model comes back with its predictions.

We know which movies Priyanka likes -- that was part of the 10% of data we held back. We can compare that against the model's predictions.

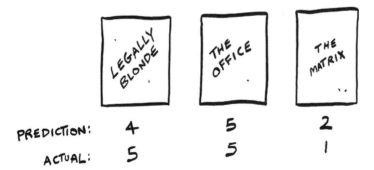

Not bad! In that case we can say the model made a good prediction, because the numbers are pretty close to Priyanka's actual ratings. This step of testing the model is called validating or evaluating the model.

After evaluating the model, we may want to go back and adjust it. For example, let's say we've built a KNN model where K = five. We may want to try it with K = seven to see if it gives better results. This is called *parameter tuning*.

After you're done training and evaluating the model, you have a model ready to go! These are the steps in building an ML model at a high level.

Recap

I hope this gives you an idea of all the different things you can do with KNN and with machine learning! Machine learning is an interesting field that you can go pretty deep into if you decide to.

- KNN is used for classification and regression and involves looking at the k-nearest neighbors.

- Classification = categorization into a group.

- Regression = predicting a response (like a number).

- Feature extraction means converting an item (like a fruit or a user) into a list of numbers that can be compared.

- Picking good features is an important part of a successful KNN algorithm.

FEATURE EXTRACTION

In this chapter

- You get a brief overview of 10 algorithms that haven't been covered in this book and why they're useful.

- You get pointers on what to read next, depending on what your interests are.

Linear regression

Suppose you need to sell your house. It is 3,000 ft². You look at the homes recently sold in your neighborhood.

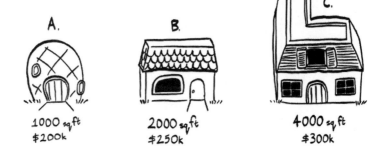

A.
1000 sq ft
$200k

B.
2000 sq ft
$250k

C.
4000 sq ft
$300k

Based on this information, how would you price your house? Here's one way you could do it. Plot all the points.

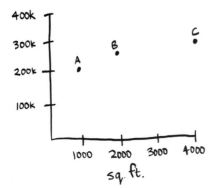

Then eyeball a line through these points.

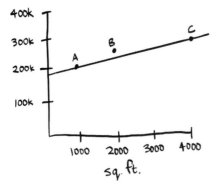

Now you can see where 3000 ft² lands on that line, and that would be a pretty good starting price for your home:

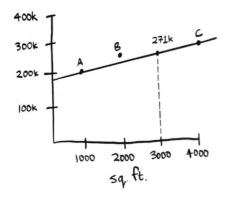

This is how linear regression works. Given a bunch of points, it tries to fit a line to them, and then you can use that line to make predictions.

Linear regression has been used in statistics for a long time, and now it is being widely used in machine learning because it is an easy first technique to try. It is useful if your values are continuous. If you are trying to predict something, linear regression might be a good place to start.

Inverted indexes

Here's a very simplified version of how a search engine works. Suppose you have three web pages with this simple content.

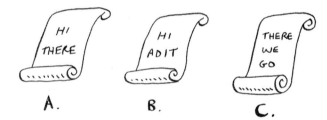

Let's build a hash table from this content.

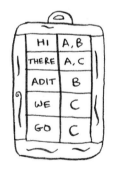

The keys of the hash table are the words, and the values tell you what pages each word appears on. Now suppose a user searches for *hi*. Let's see what pages *hi* shows up on.

Aha! It appears on pages A and B. Let's show the user those pages as the result. Or suppose the user searches for *there*. Well, you know that it shows up on pages A and C. Pretty easy, huh? This is a useful data structure: a hash that maps words to places where they appear. This data structure is called an *inverted index*, and it's commonly used to build search engines. If you're interested in search, this is a good place to start.

The Fourier transform

The Fourier transform is one of those rare algorithms: brilliant, elegant, and with a million use cases. The best analogy for the Fourier transform comes from Better Explained (a great website that explains math simply): given a smoothie, the Fourier transform will tell you the ingredients in the smoothie.[1] Or, to put it another way, given a song, the transform can separate it into individual frequencies.

It turns out that this simple idea has a lot of use cases. For example, if you can separate a song into frequencies, you can boost the ones you care about. You could boost the bass and hide the treble. The Fourier transform is great for processing signals. You can also use it to compress music. First, you break an audio file down into its ingredient notes. The Fourier transform tells you exactly how much each note contributes to the overall song. So you can get rid of the notes that aren't important. That's how the MP3 format works!

Music isn't the only type of digital signal. The JPG format is another compressed format, and it works the same way. People use the Fourier transform to try to predict upcoming earthquakes and analyze DNA. You can use it to build an app like Shazam, which guesses what song is playing. The Fourier transform has a lot of uses. Chances are high that you'll run into it!

---

[1] Kalid, "An Interactive Guide to the Fourier Transform," Better Explained, http://mng.bz/dd9N.

Parallel algorithms

The next three topics are about scalability and working with a lot of data. Back in the day, computers kept getting faster and faster. If you wanted to make your algorithm faster, you could wait a few months, and the computers themselves would become faster. But we're near the end of that period. Instead, laptops and computers ship with multiple cores. To make your algorithms faster, you need to change them to run in parallel across all the cores at once!

Here's a simple example. The best you can do with a sorting algorithm is roughly $O(n \log n)$. It's well known that you can't sort an array in $O(n)$ time—*unless you use a parallel algorithm*! There's a parallel version of quicksort that will sort an array in $O(n)$ time.

Parallel algorithms are hard to design. And it's hard to make sure they work correctly and to figure out what type of speed boost you'll see. One thing is for sure—the time gains aren't linear. So if you have two cores in your laptop instead of one, that almost never means your algorithm will magically run twice as fast. There are a couple of reasons for this:

- *Overhead of managing the parallelism*—Suppose you have to sort an array of 1,000 items. How do you divide this task between the two cores? Do you give each core 500 items to sort and then merge the two sorted arrays into one big sorted array? Merging the two arrays takes time.

- *Amdahl's law*—Suppose you are painting a picture. Paintings take you very long to do, typically 20 hours. Ideally, you would do it in 10 hours. You decide to optimize your process. You break it down into two steps: (i) doing the initial sketch and (ii) painting it. For the initial sketch, instead of free-handing it, surely tracing will be faster. But the next time you paint, it still takes 19 hours and 5 minutes! What happened? Well, the sketch used to take an hour. You've got it down to 5 minutes, which is a big improvement. But the painting is the part that took the most time, and you didn't optimize that at all.

This is Amdahl's law. Amdahl's law says that when you optimize one part of the system, the performance gain is limited by how much time that part actually takes. In this case, we cut the sketch time to 1/12th of what it used to be. In the process, we saved 55 minutes. If we could have cut the painting time by the same amount, we would have saved 1,045 minutes! When you are speeding up your algorithm by parallelizing it, think about which part to parallelize. Are you parallelizing the painting part or the sketching part?

- *Load balancing*—Suppose you have 10 tasks to do, so you give each core five tasks. But core A gets all the easy tasks, so it's done in 10 seconds, whereas core B gets all the hard tasks, so it takes a minute. That means core A was sitting idle for 50 seconds while core B was doing all the work! How do you distribute the work evenly so both cores are working equally hard?

If you're interested in the theoretical side of performance and scalability, parallel algorithms might be for you!

map/reduce

There's a special type of parallel algorithm that is becoming increasingly popular: the *distributed algorithm*. It's fine to run a parallel algorithm on your laptop if you need two to four cores, but what if you need hundreds of cores? Then you can write your algorithm to run across multiple machines. Google popularized a distributed algorithm that they called MapReduce, but these functions have been around for longer.

Why are distributed algorithms useful? Suppose you have a table with billions or trillions of rows, and you want to run a complicated SQL query on it. You can't run it on MySQL because it struggles after a few billion rows. Use map/reduce!

Or suppose you have to process a long list of jobs. Each job takes 10 seconds to process, and you need to process 1 million jobs like this. If you do this on one machine, it will take you months! If you could run it across 100 machines, you might be done in a few days.

Distributed algorithms are great when you have a lot of work to do and want to speed up the time required to do it.

Bloom filters and HyperLogLog

Suppose you're running Reddit. When someone posts a link, you want to see if it's been posted before. Stories that haven't been posted before are considered more valuable. So you need to figure out whether this link has been posted before.

Or suppose you're Google, and you're crawling web pages. You only want to crawl a web page if you haven't crawled it already. So you need to figure out whether this page has been crawled before.

Or suppose you're running bit.ly, which is a URL shortener. You don't want to redirect users to malicious websites. You have a set of URLs that are considered malicious. Now you need to figure out whether you're redirecting the user to a URL in that set.

All of these examples have the same problem. You have a very large set.

Now you have a new item, and you want to see whether it belongs in that set. You could do this quickly with a hash. For example, suppose Google has a big hash in which the keys are all the pages it has crawled.

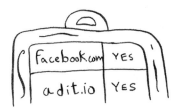

You want to see whether you've already crawled adit.io. Look it up in the hash.

$$adit.io \rightarrow YES$$

`adit.io` is a key in the hash, so you've already crawled it. The average lookup time for hash tables is O(1). `adit.io` is in the hash, so you've already crawled it. You found that out in constant time. Pretty good!

Except that this hash needs to be *huge*. Google indexes trillions of web pages. If this hash has all the URLs that Google has indexed, it will take up a lot of space. Reddit and bit.ly have the same space problem. When you have so much data, you need to get creative!

Bloom filters

Bloom filters offer a solution. Bloom filters are *probabilistic data structures*. They give you an answer that could be wrong but is probably correct. Instead of a hash, you can ask your bloom filter if you've crawled this URL before. A hash table would give you an accurate answer. A bloom filter will give you an answer that's probably correct:

- False positives are possible. Google might say, "You've already crawled this site," even though you haven't.

- False negatives aren't possible. If the bloom filter says, "You haven't crawled this site," then you *definitely* haven't crawled this site.

Bloom filters are great because they take up very little space. A hash table would have to store every URL crawled by Google, but a bloom filter doesn't have to do that. They're great when you don't need an exact answer, as in all of these examples. It's OK for bit.ly to say, "We think this site might be malicious, so be extra careful."

HyperLogLog

Along the same lines is another algorithm called HyperLogLog. Suppose Google wants to count the number of *unique* searches performed by its users. Or suppose Amazon wants to count the number of unique items that users looked at today. Answering these questions takes a lot of space! With Google, you'd have to keep a log of all the unique searches. When a user searches for something, you have to see whether it's already in the log. If not, you have to add it to the log. Even for a single day, this log would be massive!

HyperLogLog approximates the number of unique elements in a set. Just like bloom filters, it won't give you an exact answer, but it comes very close and uses only a fraction of the memory a task like this would otherwise take.

If you have a lot of data and are satisfied with approximate answers, check out probabilistic algorithms!

HTTPS and the Diffie–Hellman key exchange

HTTPS is the backbone of the internet, enabling secure online transactions from password entry to online purchases. HTTPS works by encrypting messages between the client and the server. Here's how encryption works. You pass a message and a secret key into a function. It then generates an encrypted message.

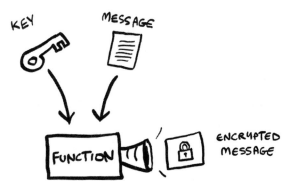

To decrypt the message, pass the encrypted message and the *same key* into a function, and you will get back the original message.

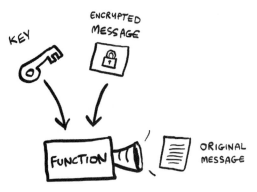

When you send some data to a server, your browser encrypts the message for you, and then the server decrypts it. Simple, right? Except for one thing: How do you make sure your browser and the server have the same key?

Remember that for HTTPS to work, both sides need to have the same key. But how do you agree on a key without someone seeing what it is? If you send the server a key to use, someone could intercept that key. How do you agree on a key so that only your browser and the server know what key you're using? This seems impossible, but it can be done! There's a very clever algorithm to do it called the Diffie–Hellman key exchange. Here's how it works.

In step 1, we generate our own keys. I'm the client, and I generate a key for myself. The server also generates a key. These keys are different. We don't know each other's keys. They are private to us.

I'm using a pattern here for each key so I can show you visually what happens. In reality, these would be bytes.

In step 2, we generate a common pattern.

This pattern is public. Both of us can see it as well as anyone else. We don't care who sees it.

In step 3, we each overlay this pattern onto our private key.

Doing so gives us our *public key*. The public key is, well, public, so we don't care who sees it. The server can see my public key, and I can see its public key.

Finally, in step 4, I take the server's public key and overlay it onto my private key. And the server does the same with my public key.

Tada! We now have the same key! We both have a key that combines three patterns.

Somehow we have both agreed on a key without ever sending the key to each other. This key we have agreed on is called the *shared secret*, and that's how the Diffie–Hellman key exchange works.

HTTPS is a fascinating and important part of our daily lives. Here are some terms you'll hear about in connection to HTTPS:

- *TLS*—TLS (Transport Layer Security) is a protocol. TLS is how we establish this secure connection.

- *SSL*—SSL is the old name for TLS, but people often don't make a distinction. If you hear someone say SSL, they are probably talking about TLS. People find security holes in these protocols, so they constantly need to be updated. The TLS protocol was first introduced in 1999. Every version of the SSL protocol that came before the TLS protocol is broken.

- *Symmetric key encryption*—In our example, both sides used the same key. There is also something called *asymmetric key encryption*, where both sides have different keys. I talked about symmetric key encryption because that is what HTTPS uses.

HTTPS uses a modified version of the Diffie–Hellman key exchange called the *ephemeral Diffie–Hellman key exchange*. It works exactly like we just saw, except the private keys are generated fresh for every connection. This means even if an attacker discovers one of the private keys, they can only decrypt the messages from one connection.

The world of cryptography is deep and interesting. If you'd like to learn more, I highly recommend another Manning book: *Real-World Cryptography* by David Wong (https://www.manning.com/books/real-world-cryptography).

Locality-sensitive hashing

A lot of hash functions you use will be locality insensitive. Suppose you have a string, and you generate a hash for it using SHA-256.

$$dog \rightarrow cd6357$$

If you change just one character of the string and regenerate the hash, it's totally different!

$$dot \rightarrow e392da$$

This is good because an attacker can't compare hashes to see whether they're close to cracking a password.

Sometimes, you want the opposite: you want a locality-sensitive hash function. That's where *Simhash* comes in. If you make a small change to a string, Simhash generates a hash that's only a little different. This allows you to compare hashes and see how similar two strings are, which is pretty useful!

- Google uses Simhash to detect duplicates while crawling the web.

- A teacher could use Simhash to see whether a student copied an essay from the web.

- Scribd allows users to upload documents or books to share with others. But Scribd doesn't want users uploading copyrighted content! The site could use Simhash to check whether an upload is similar to a *Harry Potter* book and, if so, reject it automatically.

Simhash is useful when you want to check for similar items.

Min heaps and priority queues

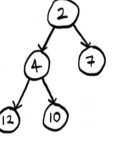

Min heaps are a data structure built using trees. These heaps store a bunch of numbers. Here is an example of a min heap.

Min heaps let you get the smallest element in the heap quickly since the smallest value is always the root. This is the main usefulness of the min heap. You can look at the smallest element in O(1) time.

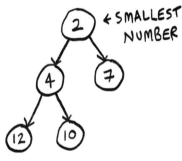

Or, in O(log *n*) time, you can remove it from the heap with a new min in its place:

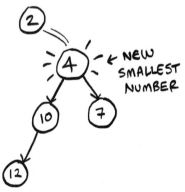

Heaps let you sort very easily. Keep asking for the minimum value.

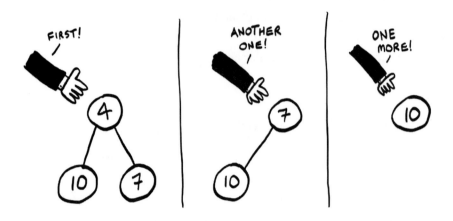

And keep putting the values in order. At the end, the tree will be empty, and you will have a sorted list of numbers! This algorithm is called *heapsort*.

Max heaps are very similar to min heaps, but now the root is the largest value.

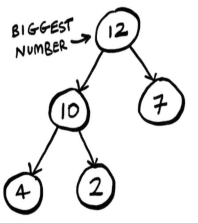

Heaps are great for implementing priority queues. We met the queue data structure in chapter 6. Remember that queues are a FIFO (first in, first out) data structure. (In contrast, a stack is a LIFO [last in, first out] data structure.) Well, a priority queue is just like a queue, except when you ask for an item, it gives you the item with the highest priority! A to-do list application is a great use case for a priority queue. First, you put in your to-dos. Then you ask for something to work on, and your priority queue gives you the next highest priority to-do. Priority queues are also used to implement an efficient version of Dijkstra's algorithm.

Linear programming

I saved the best for last. Linear programming is one of the coolest things I know.

Linear programming is used to maximize something given some linear constraints. For example, suppose your company makes two products, shirts and totes. Shirts need 1 m of fabric and five buttons. Totes need 2 m of fabric and two buttons. You have 11 meters of fabric and 20 buttons. You make $2 per shirt and $3 per tote. How many shirts and totes should you make to maximize your profit?

Here you're trying to maximize profit, and you're constrained by the amount of materials you have.

Another example: you're a politician, and you want to maximize the number of votes you get. Your research has shown that it takes an average of 1 hour of work (marketing, research, and so on) for each vote from a San Franciscan or 1.5 hours/vote from a Chicagoan. You need at least 500 San Franciscans and at least 300 Chicagoans. You have 50 days. It costs you $2/San Franciscan versus $1/Chicagoan. Your total budget is $1,500. What's the maximum number of total votes you can get (San Francisco + Chicago)?

Here you're trying to maximize votes, and you're constrained by time and money.

You might be thinking, "You've talked about a lot of optimization topics in this book. How are they related to linear programming?" All the graph algorithms we have discussed in this book can be done through linear programming instead. Linear programming is a much more general framework, and the graph problems we have seen are a subset of that. I hope your mind is blown!

Linear programming uses the Simplex algorithm. It's a complex algorithm, which is why I didn't include it in this book. If you're interested in optimization, look up linear programming!

Epilogue

I hope this quick tour of 10 algorithms showed you how much more is left to discover. I think the best way to learn is to find something you're interested in and dive in. This book gives you a solid foundation to do just that.

This appendix discusses the performance of AVL trees, which were introduced in chapter 8. You will need to read that chapter before reading this.

Remember that AVL trees offer O(log *n*) search performance. But there is something misleading going on. Here are two trees. Both offer O(log *n*) search performance, but their heights are different!

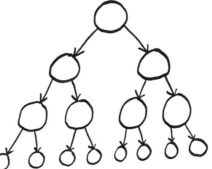

PERFECTLY BALANCED TREE
15 NODES
HEIGHT: **3**

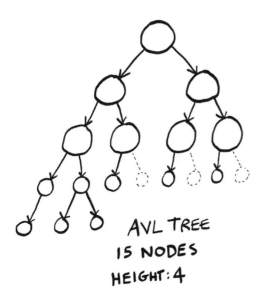

AVL TREE
15 NODES
HEIGHT: 4

(Dashed nodes show the holes in the tree.)

AVL trees allow a difference of one in heights. That's why, even though both these trees have 15 nodes, the perfectly balanced tree is height 3, but the AVL tree is height 4. The perfectly balanced tree is what we might picture a balanced tree to look like, where each level is completely filled with nodes before a new level is added. But the AVL tree is also considered "balanced," even though it has holes—gaps where a node could be.

Remember that in a tree, performance is closely related to height. How can these trees offer the same performance if their heights are different? Well, we never discussed what the base in log *n* is!

The perfectly balanced tree has performance O(log *n*), where the "log" is log base 2, just like binary search. We can see that in the picture. Each new level doubles the nodes plus 1. So a perfectly balanced tree of height 1 has 3 nodes, of height 2 has 7 nodes (32 + 1), of height 3 has 15 nodes (72 + 1), etc. You could also think of it as each layer adds a number of nodes equal to a power of 2.

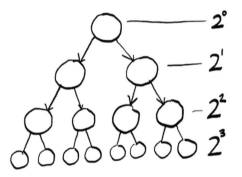

So the perfectly balanced tree has performance O(log *n*), where the "log" is log base 2.

The AVL tree has some gaps. In an AVL tree, each new layer adds *less* than double the nodes. It turns out that an AVL offers performance O(log *n*), but the "log" is log base *phi* (aka the golden ratio, aka ~1.618).

This is a small but interesting difference—AVL trees offer performance that is not quite as good as perfectly balanced trees since the base is different. But the performance is still very close, since both are O(log *n*) after all. Just know it's not exactly the same.

Both the set-covering and traveling salesperson problems have
something in common: they are hard to solve. You have to check every
possible iteration to find the smallest set cover or the shortest route.

Both of these problems are NP-hard. The terms *NP*, *NP-hard*, and *NP-
complete* can cause a lot of confusion. They certainly confused me. In
this appendix, I'll try to explain what all these terms mean, but I need
to explain some other concepts first. Here is a roadmap of the things we
will learn and how they depend on each other:

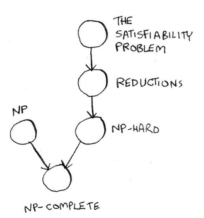

But, first, I need to explain what a *decision problem* is because
all the problems we will look at in the rest of this appendix are
decision problems.

Decision problems

NP-complete problems are always decision problems. A decision problem has a yes-or-no answer. The traveling salesperson problem is not a decision problem. It's asking you to find the shortest path, which is an optimization problem.

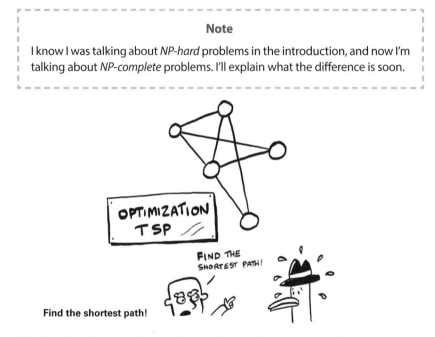

Find the shortest path!

Here's a decision version of the traveling salesperson problem.

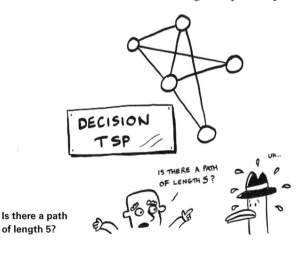

Is there a path of length 5?

Notice how this question has a yes-or-no answer: is there a path of length 5? I wanted to talk about decision problems up front because all NP-complete problems are decision problems. So *all the problems I discuss in the rest of this appendix will be decision problems.* So when you see "traveling salesperson" mentioned in the rest of this appendix, I mean the *decision* version of the traveling salesperson problem.

Now let's start learning what NP-complete actually means! The first step is to learn about the satisfiability (SAT) problem.

The satisfiability problem

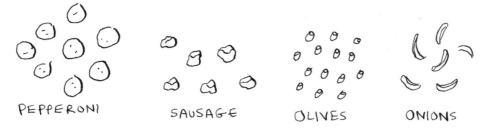

Jerry, George, Elaine, and Kramer are all ordering pizza.

"Ooh, let's get pepperoni!" says Elaine.

"Pepperoni is good. Sausage is good. We could get pepperoni or sausage," says Jerry.

"Get me an olive pizza to maintain my complexion," says Kramer. "*Lots* of olives. Or, onions."

"I can do any pizza but *no* onions," says George. "I can't take any more onions, Jerry!"

"Oh boy. OK, let me figure this out. So what toppings do I need again?" says Jerry.

Can you help him out? Here are everyone's requirements:

- Pepperoni (Elaine)

- Pepperoni or sausage (Jerry)

- Olives or onions (Kramer)

- No onions (George)

See if you can figure out what toppings the pizza should have before moving on.

Did you get it? A pepperoni and olive pizza satisfies all the requirements. This is an example of a SAT problem. In pseudocode, I could write it like this. First, I have four boolean variables:

```
pepperoni = ?
sausage = ?
olives = ?
onions = ?
```

Then I write out a boolean formula:

```
(pepperoni) and (pepperoni or sausage) and (olives or
onions) and (not onions)
```

This formula contains the requirements for each person in the form of boolean logic. The SAT problem asks the question: Can you set these variables to some values so that the statement evaluates to `true`?

The SAT problem is famous because it is the first NP-complete problem, described in 1971 (although I don't think the authors used Seinfeld as an example). Before this, the concept of an NP-complete problem did not exist. Here is how the SAT problem works. You start with a boolean formula:

```
if (pepperoni) and (olives or onions):
    print("pizza")
```

Then you ask, is there some way we can assign our variables so that code prints `pizza`?

This example is pretty easy, so we can solve it ourselves. If `pepperoni` and `onions` are `true`, this code will print `pizza`. So the answer would be *yes*.

Here's one where the answer would be *no*:

```
if (olives or onions) and (not olives) and (not onions):
    print("pizza")
```

There is nothing you can set the variables to so this code will print `pizza`!

The SAT problem always looks for a yes-or-no answer, so it is a *decision* problem.

SAT is actually a pretty hard problem. Here is a tougher example just to give you an idea:

```
if (pepperoni or not olives) and (onions or not
pepperoni) and (not olives or not pepperoni):
   print("pizza")
```

You don't need to solve this one. I'm just showing it as an example so you can appreciate how hard this problem can get. You can have any number of variables and any number of clauses, and the problems get pretty hard pretty quickly.

With n toppings, there are 2^n possible pizzas. If you list them all out and check each one, you get something called a truth table. Here's the truth table for `pepperoni and (olives or onions)`.

Sometimes you need to list every option, just like the set-covering problem and the traveling salesperson problem! In fact, the SAT problem is just as hard as these two problems. It has a big O run time of $O(2^n)$.

PEPPERONI	OLIVES	ONIONS	ANSWER
F	F	T	NO
F	T	F	NO
F	T	T	NO
T	F	F	NO
T	F	T	YES
T	T	F	YES
T	T	T	YES
F	F	F	NO

PEPPERONI AND
(OLIVES OR ONIONS)

Hard to solve, quick to verify

We often see problems where finding a solution is much harder than verifying a solution. Suppose I ask you to come up with a sentence that is a palindrome (it reads the same backward and forward) that includes the words *cat* and *car*. How long do you think it would take you to come up with that sentence?

Now suppose I tell you that I know a sentence like that. Here it is: *Was it a car or a cat I saw?*

It would take you much less time to verify that claim than to come up with your own sentence. Verifying was quicker than solving!

A SAT problem is as hard to solve as the set-covering problem or the traveling salesperson problem, but unlike those problems, verifying a solution is easy. For example, for this question that we gave earlier: (pepperoni or not olives) and (onions or not pepperoni) and (not olives or not pepperoni), here's a solution:

```
pepperoni = False
olives = False
onions = False
```

You can quickly check for yourself that these values will make that boolean formula `true`. Checking those values was faster than solving it yourself!

The SAT problem is *quick to verify*, so it is in NP.

NP is the class of problems that can be *verified* in polynomial time. NP problems may or may not be easy to solve, but they are easy to verify. This is different from P.

NP

P

A problem is in P if it can be *verified and solved* in polynomial time.

Polynomial time means its big O is not bigger than a polynomial. I won't define what a polynomial is in this book, but here's two polynomials.

$$n^3 \qquad n^2 + n$$

And here are a couple of examples that are not polynomials.

$$n! \qquad 2^n$$

P is a subset of NP. So NP contains all the problems in P, plus others.

P vs. NP

You may have heard of the famous *P versus NP* problem. We just saw that the problems in P are both quick to verify and quick to solve. The problems in NP are quick to verify but may or may not be quick to solve. The P versus NP problem asks whether every problem that is quick to verify *is also quick to solve*. If that is the case, P wouldn't be a subset of NP; P would equal NP.

NP-hard is the next term we will define, but first we need to (briefly) discuss what a reduction is.

Reductions

What do you do when you have a hard problem? Change the problem to one you can solve! In real life, when we're faced with a hard problem, it is extremely common to change the problem.

Here's one you can try right now. How do you multiply two binary numbers? Try multiplying these two binary numbers:

```
101 * 110
```

If you're like me, you didn't try to figure out how to do the multiplication in binary. You just figured out that 101 is 5 in decimal and 110 is 6, and then you multiplied 5 and 6 instead.

This is called a reduction. You are reducing a problem that you don't know how to solve to a problem you do know how to solve. This is done all the time in computer science.

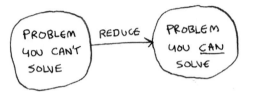

NP-hard

We have already seen three examples of NP-hard problems:

- The set-covering problem

- The traveling salesperson problem

- The SAT problem

(Remember, I mean the *decision* versions of these problems—all the problems we look at in the rest of this appendix are decision problems.)

The three previously noted problems are NP-hard. We say a problem is NP-hard *if any problem in NP can be reduced to that problem*. This is the definition of NP-hard.

You can also reduce all NP problems to any NP-hard problem. For example, you can reduce all NP problems to SAT.

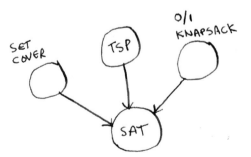

One extra requirement is that you need to be able to reduce all these problems *in polynomial time.* That "in polynomial time" is important because you don't want the reducing part to be the bottleneck. Any NP problem can be reduced to SAT in polynomial time, so it is NP-hard.

Since any problem in NP can be reduced to any NP-hard problem, a polynomial time solution for any one NP-hard problem gives us a polynomial time solution for every problem in NP!

NP-complete

We've seen two definitions:

- Problems in NP are quick to verify and may or may not be quick to solve.

- Problems that are NP-hard are at least as hard as the hardest problems in NP, and any problem in NP can be reduced to a problem in NP-hard.

Now here's my final definition: *a problem is NP-complete if it is both NP and NP-hard.*

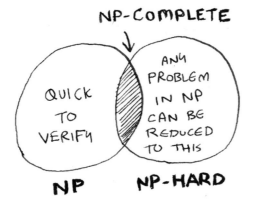

NP-complete problems are

- Hard to solve (at least right now; if someone proves that P = NP, they would not be)

- Easy to verify

And any problem in NP can be reduced to a problem that is NP-complete.

Here are the terms we defined in this appendix:

- Decision problems

- The SAT problem

- P versus NP

- Reductions

- NP-hard

- NP-complete

When you see a discussion about NP-complete problems, I hope you'll feel more confident about what these terms mean!

Recap

- A problem is in P if it is both quick to solve and quick to verify.

- A problem is in NP if it is quick to verify. It may or may not be quick to solve.

- If we find a fast (polynomial time) algorithm for every problem in NP, then P = NP.

- A problem is NP-hard if any problem in NP can be reduced to that problem.

- If a problem is in both NP and NP-hard, it is NP-complete.

CHAPTER 1

1.1 Suppose you have a sorted list of 128 names, and you're searching through it using binary search. What's the maximum number of steps it would take?

Answer: 7.

1.2 Suppose you double the size of the list. What's the maximum number of steps now?

Answer: 8.

1.3 You have a name, and you want to find the person's phone number in the phone book.

Answer: O(log n).

1.4 You have a phone number, and you want to find the person's name in the phone book. (Hint: You'll have to search through the whole book!)

Answer: O(n).

1.5 You want to read the numbers of every person in the phone book.

Answer: O(n).

1.6 You want to read the numbers of just the *A*s.

Answer: O(n). You may think, "I'm only doing this for 1 out of 26 characters, so the run time should be O(n/26)." A simple rule to remember is to ignore numbers that are added, subtracted, multiplied, or divided. None of these are correct big O run times: O(n + 26), O(n – 26), O(n * 26), O(n/26). They're all the same as

O(*n*)! Why? If you're curious, flip to "big O notation revisited" in chapter 4 and read up on constants in big O notation (a constant is just a number; 26 was the constant in this question).

CHAPTER 2

2.1   Suppose you're building an app to keep track of your finances.

1. GROCERIES
2. MOVIE
3. SFBC MEMBERSHIP

Every day, you write down everything you spent money on. At the end of the month, you review your expenses and sum up how much you spent. So, you have lots of inserts and a few reads. Should you use an array or a list?

Answer: In this case, you're adding expenses to the list every day and reading all the expenses once a month. Arrays have fast reads and slow inserts. Linked lists have slow reads and fast inserts. Because you'll be inserting more often than reading, it makes sense to use a linked list. Also, linked lists have slow reads only if you're accessing random elements in the list. Because you're reading *every* element in the list, linked lists will do well on *reads*, too. So a linked list is a good solution to this problem.

2.2   Suppose you're building an app for restaurants to take customer orders. Your app needs to store a list of orders. Servers keep adding orders to this list, and chefs take orders off the list and make them. It's an order queue: servers add orders to the back of the queue, and the chef takes the first order off the queue and cooks it.

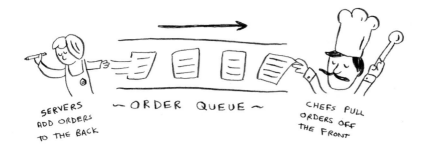

SERVERS
ADD ORDERS
TO THE BACK   — ORDER   QUEUE ~   CHEFS PULL
ORDERS OFF
THE FRONT

Would you use an array or a linked list to implement this queue? (Hint: Linked lists are good for inserts/deletes, and arrays are good for random access. Which one are you going to be doing here?)

Answer: A linked list. Lots of inserts are happening (servers adding orders), which linked lists excel at. You don't need search or random access (what arrays excel at) because the chefs always take the first order off the queue.

2.3 Let's run a thought experiment. Suppose Facebook keeps a list of usernames. When someone tries to log in to Facebook, a search is done for their username. If their name is in the list of usernames, they can log in. People log in to Facebook pretty often, so there are a lot of searches through this list of usernames. Suppose Facebook uses binary search to search the list. Binary search needs random access—you need to be able to get to the middle of the list of usernames instantly. Knowing this, would you implement the list as an array or a linked list?

Answer: A sorted array. Arrays give you random access—you can get an element from the middle of the array instantly. You can't do that with linked lists. To get to the middle element in a linked list, you'd have to start at the first element and follow all the links down to the middle element.

2.4 People sign up for Facebook pretty often, too. Suppose you decided to use an array to store the list of users. What are the downsides of an array for inserts? In particular, suppose you're using binary search to search for logins. What happens when you add new users to an array?

Answer: Inserting into arrays is slow. Also, if you're using binary search to search for usernames, the array needs to be sorted. Suppose someone named Adit B signs up for Facebook. Their name will be inserted at the end of the array. So you need to sort the array every time a name is inserted!

2.5   In reality, Facebook uses neither an array nor a linked list to store
user information. Let's consider a hybrid data structure: an array
of linked lists. You have an array with 26 slots. Each slot points to a
linked list. For example, the first slot in the array points to a linked
list containing all the usernames starting with *A*. The second slot
points to a linked list containing all the usernames starting with *B*,
and so on.

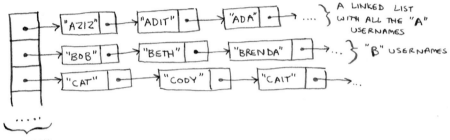

AN ARRAY

Suppose Adit B signs up for Facebook, and you want to add them
to the list. You go to slot 1 in the array, go to the linked list for slot
1, and add Adit B at the end. Now, suppose you want to search for
Zakhir H. You go to slot 26, which points to a linked list of all the
Z names. Then you search through that list to find Zakhir H.

Compare this hybrid data structure to arrays and linked lists. Is it
slower or faster than each for searching and inserting? You don't
have to give big O run times, just whether the new data structure
would be faster or slower.

Answer: Searching—slower than arrays, faster than linked lists.
Inserting—faster than arrays, same amount of time as linked lists.
So it's slower for searching than an array, but faster or the same as
linked lists for everything. We'll talk about another hybrid data
structure called a hash table later in the book. This should give you
an idea of how you can build up more complex data structures
from simple ones.

So what does Facebook really use? It probably uses a dozen
different databases with different data structures behind them:
hash tables, B-trees, and others. Arrays and linked lists are the
building blocks for these more complex data structures.

CHAPTER 3

3.1   Suppose I show you a call stack like this.

What information can you give me, just based on this call stack?

Answer: Here are some things you could tell me:

The greet function is called first, with name = maggie.

Then the greet function calls the greet2 function, with name = maggie.

At this point, the greet function is in an incomplete, suspended state.

The current function call is the greet2 function.

After this function call completes, the greet function will resume.

3.2   Suppose you accidentally write a recursive function that runs forever. As you saw, your computer allocates memory on the stack for each function call. What happens to the stack when your recursive function runs forever?

Answer: The stack grows forever. Each program has a limited amount of space on the call stack. When your program runs out of space (which it eventually will), it will exit with a stack-overflow error.

CHAPTER 4

4.1 Write out the code for the earlier sum function.

Answer:

```
def sum(list):
  if list == []:
    return 0
  return list[0] + sum(list[1:])
```

4.2 Write a recursive function to count the number of items in a list.

Answer:

```
def count(list):
  if list == []:
    return 0
  return 1 + count(list[1:])
```

4.3 Write a recursive function to find the maximum number in a list.

Answer:

```
def max(list):
  if len(list) == 2:
    return list[0] if list[0] > list[1] else list[1]
  sub_max = max(list[1:])
  return list[0] if list[0] > sub_max else sub_max
```

4.4 Remember binary search from chapter 1? It's a D&C algorithm, too. Can you come up with the base case and recursive case for binary search?

Answer: The base case for binary search is an array with one item. If the item you're looking for matches the item in the array, you found it! Otherwise, it isn't in the array.

In the recursive case for binary search, you split the array in half, throw away one half, and call binary search on the other half.

How long would each of these operations take in big O notation?

4.5 Printing the value of each element in an array.

Answer: O(*n*)

4.6 Doubling the value of each element in an array.

Answer: O(*n*)

4.7 Doubling the value of just the first element in an array.

Answer: O(1)

4.8 Creating a multiplication table with all the elements in the array. So if your array is [2, 3, 7, 8, 10], you first multiply every element by 2, then multiply every element by 3, then by 7, and so on.

Answer: $O(n^2)$

CHAPTER 5

Which of these hash functions are consistent?

5.1 `f(x) = 1` ◄·········· **Returns 1 for all input**

Answer: Consistent

5.2 `f(x) = rand()` ◄·········· **Returns a random number every time**

Answer: Not consistent

5.3 `f(x) = next_empty_slot()` ◄·········· **Returns the index of the next empty slot in the hash table**

Answer: Not consistent

5.4 `f(x) = len(x)` ◄·········· **Uses the length of the string as the index**

Answer: Consistent

Suppose you have these four hash functions that work with strings:

A. Return "1" for all input.

B. Use the length of the string as the index.

C. Use the first character of the string as the index. So, all strings starting with *a* are hashed together, and so on.

D. Map every letter to a prime number: a = 2, b = 3, c = 5, d = 7, e = 11, and so on. For a string, the hash function is the sum of all the characters modulo the size of the hash. For example, if your hash size is 10, and the string is "bag," the index is 3 + 2 + 17 % 10 = 22 % 10 = 2.

For each of the following examples, which hash functions would provide a good distribution? Assume a hash table size of 10 slots.

5.5 A phonebook where the keys are names and values are phone numbers. The names are as follows: Esther, Ben, Bob, and Dan.

Answer: Hash functions C and D would give a good distribution.

5.6   A mapping from battery size to power. The sizes are A, AA, AAA, and AAAA.

Answer: Hash functions B and D would give a good distribution.

5.7   A mapping from book titles to authors. The titles are *Maus, Fun Home,* and *Watchmen.*

Answer: Hash functions B, C, and D would give a good distribution.

CHAPTER 6

Run the breadth-first search algorithm on each of these graphs to find the solution.

6.1   Find the length of the shortest path from start to finish.

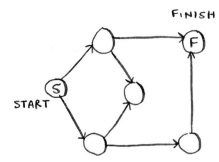

Answer: The shortest path has a length of 2.

6.2   Find the length of the shortest path from "cab" to "bat."

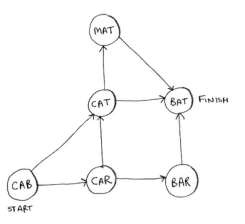

Answer: The shortest path has a length of 2.

Here's a small graph of my morning routine.

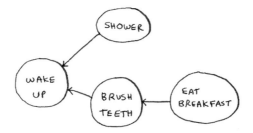

6.3 For these three lists, mark whether each one is valid or invalid.

A.	**B.**	**C.**
1. WAKE UP	1. WAKE UP	1. SHOWER
2. SHOWER	2. BRUSH TEETH	2. WAKE UP
3. EAT BREAKFAST	3. EAT BREAKFAST	3. BRUSH TEETH
4. BRUSH TEETH	4. SHOWER	4. EAT BREAKFAST

Answers: A—Invalid; B—Valid; C—Invalid.

6.4 Here's a larger graph. Make a valid list for this graph.

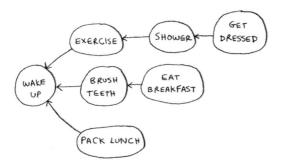

Answer: 1—Wake up; 2—Exercise; 3—Shower; 4—Brush teeth; 5—Get dressed; 6—Pack lunch; 7—Eat breakfast.

6.5 Which of the following graphs are also trees?

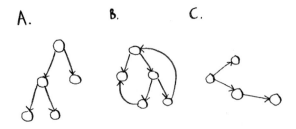

A.   B.   C.

Answers: A—Tree; B—Not a tree; C—Tree. The last example is just a sideways tree. Trees are a subset of graphs. So a tree is always a graph, but a graph may or may not be a tree.

CHAPTER 9

9.1 In each of these graphs, what is the weight of the shortest path from Start to Finish?

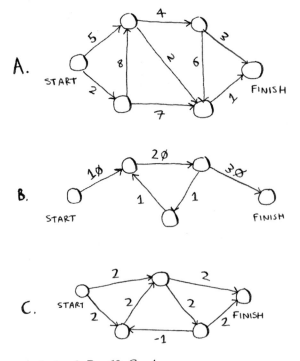

Answers: A: A—8; B—60; C—4.

CHAPTER 10

10.1 You work for a furniture company, and you have to ship furniture all over the country. You need to pack your truck with boxes. All the boxes are of different sizes, and you're trying to maximize the space you use in each truck. How would you pick boxes to maximize space? Come up with a greedy strategy. Will that give you the optimal solution?

Answer: A greedy strategy would be to pick the largest box that will fit in the remaining space and repeat until you can't pack any more boxes. No, this won't give you the optimal solution.

10.2 You're going to Europe, and you have seven days to see everything you can. You assign a point value to each item (how much you want to see it) and estimate how long it takes. How can you maximize the point total (seeing all the things you really want to see) during your stay? Come up with a greedy strategy. Will that give you the optimal solution?

Answer: Keep picking the activity with the highest point value that you can still do in the time you have left. Stop when you can't do anything else. No, this won't give you the optimal solution.

CHAPTER 11

11.1 Suppose you can steal another item: a mechanical keyboard. It weighs 1 lb and is worth $1,000. Should you steal it?

Answer: Yes. Then you could steal the mechanical keyboard, the iPhone, and the guitar, worth a total of $4,500.

11.2 Suppose you're going camping. You have a knapsack that holds 6 lb, and you can take the following items. They each have a value, and the higher the value, the more important the item is:

- Water, 3 lb, 10

- Book, 1 lb, 3

- Food, 2 lb, 9

- Jacket, 2 lb, 5

- Camera, 1 lb, 6

What's the optimal set of items to take on your camping trip?

Answer: You should take water, food, and a camera.

11.3 Draw and fill in the grid to calculate the longest common substring between *blue* and *clues*.

Answer:

	C	L	U	E	S
B	0	0	0	0	0
L	0	1	0	0	0
U	0	0	2	0	0
E	0	0	0	3	0

CHAPTER 12

12.1 In the Netflix example, you calculated the distance between two different users using the distance formula. But not all users rate movies the same way. Suppose you have two users, Yogi and Pinky, who have the same taste in movies. But Yogi rates any movie he likes as a 5, whereas Pinky is choosier and reserves the 5s for only the best. They're well matched, but according to the distance algorithm, they aren't neighbors. How would you take their different rating strategies into account?

Answer: You could use something called normalization. You look at the average rating for each person and use it to scale their ratings. For example, you might notice that Pinky's average rating is 3, whereas Yogi's average rating is 3.5. So you bump up Pinky's ratings a little until her average rating is 3.5 as well. Then you can compare their ratings on the same scale.

12.2 Suppose Netflix nominates a group of "influencers." For example, Quentin Tarantino and Wes Anderson are influencers on Netflix, so their ratings count for more than a normal user's. How would you change the recommendations system so it's biased toward the ratings of influencers?

Answer: You could give more weight to the ratings of the influencers when using KNN. Suppose you have three neighbors: Joe, Dave, and Wes Anderson (an influencer). They rated Caddyshack 3, 4, and 5, respectively. Instead of just taking the average of their ratings (3 + 4 + 5 / 3 = 4 stars), you could give Wes Anderson's rating more weight: 3 + 4 + 5 + 5 + 5 / 5 = 4.4 stars.

12.3 Netflix has millions of users. The earlier example looked at the five closest neighbors for building the recommendations system. Is this too low? Too high?

Answer: It's too low. If you look at fewer neighbors, there's a bigger chance that the results will be skewed. A good rule of thumb is that if you have N users, you should look at sqrt(N) neighbors.

index

A

algorithms
    running times of, growth rates of 11–13
    run-time analysis, worst-case run time 15
approximate solution 205
approximation algorithms 197
arrays
    linked lists and 24–25
    terminology 27
ASCII (American Standard Code for Information Interchange) 134
asymmetric key encryption 259
average case 70
    quicksort, vs. worst case 75
AVL trees 151

B

balanced trees 141, 150, 164
    AVL trees 151
    B-trees 162–164
    improving insertion speed with 143
    rotation 151
    splay trees 159
balance factor 154
base case, in recursion 44–45
Bellman-Ford algorithm 180

BFS (breadth-first search) 101, 120
    graphs, overview of 102–104
    implementing BFS algorithm 113–117
    implementing graph 111–112
    overview of 106, 109
    shortest path problem, using breadth-first search 108–109
Big O notation 10, 75
    average case vs. worst case 72–75
    establishing worst-case run time 15
    merge sort vs. quicksort 71–72
    run times 15–17, 70
    traveling salesperson problem 17–19
    visualizing run times 13
binary search 3, 142
    running time of 10
binary_search function 8
binary search trees (BSTs) 143
binary trees 131, 139
Bloom filters 253
breadth-first search. *See* BFS (breadth-first search)
brute-force algorithms, knapsack problem 204
BSTs. *See* binary search trees
B-trees 161
    advantages of 162–164
bye function 48

C

cache, using hash tables as 88
call stack 46, 47–49, 49
character encoding 134
collisions 91–93
connected, acyclic graph 130
constant 71
constant time 94
countdown example, base case and recursive case 44–45

D

data structures
    arrays
        linked lists and 24–25
        overview of 26
        selection sort and 24
        terminology 27
    AVL trees 151
    balanced trees 147–150, 164
    binary search trees (BSTs) 143
    binary trees 131, 139
    B-trees 161
    graphs
        BFS, implementing 111–112
        Dijkstra's algorithm, implementation of 181–189
        overview of 102–105, 122
        terminology 170–172
        weighted 165

data structures (*continued*)
   hash tables 77, 84, 91, 99, 111
   heaps 261–263
   linked lists 24
   probabilistic algorithms, Hyper-
      LogLog 255
   queues, overview of 109
   recommendation systems 231
   splay trees 159
   stacks
      call stack 47–49
      call stack with recursion
         49–53
   trees, depth-first search 126–129
D&C. *See* divide and conquer
   (D&C)
decision problems 268
deletions 30
depth-first search (DFS) 126–129
deque function 113
dictionaries 83
diff command 227
Diffie-Hellman key exchange 255
   ephemeral Diffie-Hellman key
      exchange 259
Dijkstra's algorithm 165, 190
   implementation of 181–189
   terminology 170–172
   working with 166–170
directed graph 112
distributed algorithms 252
divide and conquer (D&C) 56–63
   quicksort 64–76
DNS cache 86
DNS resolution 86
duplicates, preventing 86–88
dynamic programming 228
   knapsack problem 203, 216
      brute-force solution 204
      dynamic programming solu-
         tion for 205
      FAQ 213, 216, 217
      filling in grid 216
      filling knapsack completely
         220
      items that depend on each
         other 219

overview of 206–208
   stealing fractions of items
      217
longest common substring
   problem 220
   filling in grid 222–223
   longest common subse-
      quence 225
   solution 224–225

E

edges, negative-weight 178–180
enqueue 113
Euclids algorithm 58

F

factorial function 49
feature extraction 233–237, 243,
   246
Feynman algorithm 222
FIFO (first in, first out) 110, 263
file directories 123–125
find_lowest_cost_node algorithm
   184
Fourier transform 250
fruit classification example 229

G

golden ratio 266
graphs
   BFS, implementing 111–112
   Dijkstra's algorithm, implemen-
      tation of 181–189
   overview of 102–105, 122
   terminology 170–172
   weighted 165
greedy algorithms 191, 202
   knapsack problem 194–196
   set-covering problem 196–197,
      201–202
      calculating answer 199
      code for setup 198
      sets 201
greet2 function 48

greet function 48, 49
growth rates of algorithms 11–13
guitar row 206–208

H

hash functions 97
hash tables 77, 84, 91, 99, 111
   collisions 91–93
   lookups 84–86
   performance 93–95
      hash functions 97
      load factor 96–97
      preventing duplicate entries
         86–88
   use cases, lookups 84–86
   using as cache 88
heapsort algorithm 262
Huffman coding 136, 133–139
HyperLogLog 253, 255

I

inductive proofs 69
injective function 83
in-neighbors 105
ISO-8859-1 code 133

K

knapsack problem 194–196, 203
   adding items to 213–215
   adding smaller item 216
   changing order of rows 216
   dynamic programming solution
      for 205
   FAQ 213
   filling in grid row-wise 216
   filling knapsack completely 220
   items that depend on each other
      219
   optimizing travel itinerary 217
   overview of dynamic program-
      ming 206–208
   revisited, brute-force solution
      204
   stealing fractions of items 217

k-nearest neighbors (KNN) 229
 building spam filters, Naive
  Bayes classifier 243
 overview of machine learning
  241
 recommendation system
  feature extraction 233–237
  features for 240
  regression 238–240
 stock market, predicting 244
 training models, high-level overview of 224–228, 229–246

L

Levenshtein distance 227
LIFO (last in, first out) 110, 263
linear programming 263
linear regression 247
linear time 15
linked lists 24
 deletions 30
 selection sort 25, 31–34
 terminology 27
load factor 96–97
logarithmic time. *See* log time
logarithms 7
log time 10, 15
longest common substring problem 220
 filling in grid 222–223
 longest common subsequence
  225
 making grid 221–222
 solution 224–225
LSH (locality-sensitive hashing)
 260–261

M

machine learning, overview of
 241
map function 252
map/reduce 252
merge sort 70
 vs. quicksort 71–72
min heaps 261–263

ML (machine learning)
 stock market, predicting
  244
 training models, high-level
  overview of 244–246

N

Naive Bayes classifier 243
negative-weight edges 178–180
nondeterministic polynomial time
 (NP) 267
NP-complete problems 267, 268,
 275–276
NP-hard problems 267, 274–275
 hard to solve, quick to verify
  272
 overview of 274–275
 reductions 273
 satisfiability problem 269–271
NP (nondeterministic polynomial
 time) 267

O

optical character recognition
 (OCR) 242
out-neighbors 105

P

parallel algorithms 251
partitioning 65
perfect hash function 83
performance 2
pivot 64
pointers 30
pop 113
power set 196
print function 47
priority queues 261–263
probabilistic algorithms,
 HyperLogLog 255
probabilistic data structures
 254
push 113
P vs. NP problem 273

Q

queue data structure 109
quicksort 64–76
 average case vs. worst case 72–75
 Big O notation 75
 divide and conquer 56–63
 merge sort vs. 71–72
 run times for 70

R

Real-World Cryptography (Wong)
 260
recommendation systems 231
 feature extraction 233–237
recursion 41, 44, 54
 base case and recursive case 44
 call stack 47–49
 overview of 42
 stacks, call stack with recursion
  49–53
reduce function 252
reductions 273
regression 239
regression analysis, linear 247
regression, KNN (k-nearest neighbors) 238–240
rotation, in AVL trees 151, 154
run-time analysis, worst-case run
 time 15
run times 15–17
 visualizing 13

S

SAT (satisfiability) problem
 269–271
search, binary search 5–9
selection sort 21, 34, 38, 39
 arrays and linked lists 24, 31
  terminology 27
 arrays, overview of 26
 deletions 30
 insertion sort, inserting into
  middle of list 29
 memory 22–23

selection sort, code listing 38
set-covering problem 196, 267
   calculating answer 199
   code for setup 198
   greedy algorithms for
     approximation algorithms 197
shortest path 178
shortest-path algorithms, Dijkstra's
   algorithm 165
shortest-path problem 104
   terminology 170–172
   using breadth-first search
     108–109
simple search 5
spam filters, building with KNN 243
splay trees 159
stack data structure 46
stacks
   call stack 47–49
   call stack with recursion 49–53
stat command 133

subproblem 215
sum function 61, 63
symmetric key encryption 259

T

tail recursion 53
topological sort 118
training 243
traveling salesperson problem
   17–19, 267
travel itinerary, optimizing
   217
tree algorithms, file directories
   123–125
tree insertion, improving speed
   with 143
trees 119, 121, 140
   depth-first search 126–129
   Huffman coding 133–139
   overview of 122

U

unweighted graphs 170
UTF-8 (Unicode Transformation
   Format 8) 134

V

vectors 236

W

weighted graphs 170
weights 170
Wong, David, *Real-World
   Cryptography* 260
worst case 70